The Velveting Bones

Also by Liezel Graham

POETRY

Stripped
A Counting of Love

The Velveting Bones

Liezel Graham

Quiet Rebel Press

Published by Quiet Rebel Press

**First published in paperback in Great Britain in 2022
by Quiet Rebel Press**

ISBN: 978 1 9196532 6 6

Typeset in Garamond 11 point

Cover photography by Liezel Graham
Cover design by Quiet Rebel Press

www.liezelgraham.com

for **Noah Daniel**

you are a gentle king with the heart of a tender warrior

Contents

Preface

I have always found it uncomfortable to refer to myself as a poet—*storyteller,* is a far more apt description, and so this is actually a collection of intimate stories, although many wear poem-shaped coats.

They are a series of small confessions that attempt to tell of a life of many second chances.

The words were born in different seasons and over many years. My stories seldom describe only one moment in time. They are stitched together into layers, drawn from a lifetime of experiences and observations.

I wrestled with each piece, from writing it as vulnerably as I could, to whether it deserved a space in this book.

I hope that I have shaped the bones well.

If nothing else, they are honest and true.

The themes are often repeated. This simply reflects life.

The world is at times a terrifying place and each of us will encounter unbodied tragedy that will claw at everything we hold as our foundation, but there is also beauty all around us. It is the antidote to the sharp things that cause us to lose our hope. Look for it wherever you go. It always satisfies.

I talk of God in an unconventional way. This is my faith. It is blended with a deep respect for, and an honouring of, the old ways. I hope that whatever you believe, or not, you will find the simple thread of light in each word.

May you be reminded that you have always been loved.

This is the tender work that I want my words to do.

you ask what i want to do with my life

a quiet dare
the cartilage softly arching over its pulse
—the weight of it
how it fills my cupped hands, tastes like honey
sun-warmed and gritty, the unexpected sweetness
the wonder that lingers

this is what i want to do:

i want to know the earth—walk with feet bare
searching for holy things hidden low in the moss
the astonishment wrapped up in the song of the blackbird
the certain prophecy of an acorn
the hundreds of small wombs
the life
there for any soft body that wants to see

i want to teach myself how to fold the word
trust
over and over, with my brave hands
until it is shaped like a tiny gift
my fragrance clinging to it

and after each storm
you
holding your life out to me—an offering

two small coins.

a naked gospel

if i were a god and i called myself, *love*, i would pull back the lacy lounge curtains every now and then, as i go about my godly duties, just to look out for you.

in the afternoon, with my hungry ears waiting at the open kitchen window, i would listen for the familiar sound of your footsteps. even before you were born, i knew their rhythm. i would send my searching eyes down the road to the corner where the cool kids hang out after school. there where they all smoke their cheap cigarettes, their eggshell hearts secretly hoping for something that tastes like belonging. like home.

on cold, wintery days when the brimming clouds throw their buckets of water sideways at the wind, i would pull on my old floral raincoat, my hands full of fresh hope. i would wait for you at the bus stop in the rain and when you step off the number two bus, world-weary and beaten, mine will be the first smiling face that you see.

i would call for you whenever i walk past your back door:

hey! are you there? do you want to go for a walk?

not just in the slow-ticking cool of summer evenings, but on velvety, peach-skinned mornings too.

i would watch you as you sleep, my fingers counting each breath that i have given you, just to make sure that they are all there. and then, before i climb out of the window, i would lean in close and kiss your forehead tenderly.

i would leave hints of my fragrance on your hair; my maker's mark, so that bad things, evil things, would not easily find you.

but if they do, and you are afraid, it is ok. trust me. stay very still, a fallow deer, flanks wide open in the face of the hunter. i have seen this before. i know what to do. allow yourself to eat the heavy silence in small, fierce mouthfuls. do not look to the left, or to the right.

do this, and you will hear my voice saying:

don't be afraid. come with me. this is the way home. it's going to be ok. i am here with you. you are not alone. i will not leave you.

don't you know that your name is a skin-soft prophecy that has always lived inside my mouth? the honeyed sweetness of it never disappoints. if you have been told anything else, it is a lie.

with my peaty, moss-green voice, i would say things that cut straight through the clanging, straight through the holy noise that always tries to follow you, that always tries to distract you from my face:

see! you look just like me—the way that your hips flare fertile and rich. the round of your breasts. the promise of your belly. your ripe thighs. when you look in the mirror, you will see me. when you look at a stranger, you will see me. when you look at your enemy, you will see me. do not forget this. it is important. look! see how your face lives at peace within the country of my eyes.

and when you come around to visit, when you knock on my

open door with your begging-bowl hands full of someone else's hand-me-down shame, already my wrinkled god-arms would be waiting, stretched out from east to west, the soft skin of my underarms flapping with flabby joy!

let me tell you i would be a most undignified sight, swaying my hips to the sound of the radio, in my old housecoat!
i would say:

look at you, nurturing all this fear and regret, dragging guilt by the hand, trying so desperately to keep it well-fed and alive. i did not give you this! why do you hold onto it? it does not need to live.

do you think i would ask for a permission slip? for proof of identity, or a certificate of acceptance to the holy club?

perhaps you think that what i want from you is a pledge of allegiance—a smooth exchange of guilt for grace, whilst you live your life on bleeding knees. something to soothe a fragile ego that tastes like anger, and smells like war? no. no. no.

if i were a god and i called myself, *love*—i would make sure that i always had your favourite tea in the cupboard. your favourite meal would be on the range, warm and ready to be dished up. your bed would have soft sheets, laundered and smelling of young fern leaves, and seated at the fire, with my nose in a book, i would wait until you were ready, until you found all the sure-footed, soft signs leading you home.
on that day, upon your arrival, i would say:

there you are! i have missed you so much! i see you have brought some guilt with you. please put all of it down. leave it outside. yes, right there by the bins. don't bring it in. there's no place for it here. come! come inside—out of the cold with you! come and sit down by the fire with me. sit here in the comfortable chair, just mind the cat. do you mind me knitting whilst we catch up? you're just in time! there's freshly baked bread and dinner is ready. hmmm! smell that! oh, i am so glad you are home! pass me your cup, and let's have some tea.

grace gets its hands dirty

when all the soft bodies that i love are finally asleep
i hold my right ear close to the liminal boundary
between this world and the other
my mouth listening for the sound of God's footsteps
in my home
my life always hungry for a generous portion of grace
how its hands are always dirty
always digging deep
in places where the holy fear to tread.

things that bind

i am not here to tell you how to live your life.

i am here to tell about mine.

the bones are the same
and the pulse, quietly making love to the inside of the wrist
—the faithful kiss of it in the notch of the neck, even as
strangers we share this—you and i.

i tell my stories so that we don't forget because we forget
the things that call us to each other.

this is always a loss.

every day i take all the words that i own, shaping them
into gentle provocations, the sting of which i have already
removed. only the stimulus remains. the record of it.

always, i hope that someone might stumble over it, be
forced to sit down, be forced to see what lies at their feet.

—to see a thing that they have never seen before, perhaps
another life. the singular stories that litter the bones of
other humans. the courage of the telling. the beauty of it.
and behind it all, the invitation—a willingness
to draw close.

admittedly, here i am speaking of leaning in, of inclining the
head, of unbuttoning the chest, of opening the heart.

it is easy to look away, especially when the edges are too
sharp, but listen, somebody has lived a life that you
will never have to.

the magnitude of this, the grace of it, the not knowing the
exact shape of another's life unless they choose
to give it to you.

unless you *choose* to receive it from their mouth.

again, a gentle provocation.

but thank goodness for words and their shadows, for
stories that breathe long after we have left.
these are the things that we leave behind.

today the sky was a small promise. for a moment, empty
of all its water, it was big and blue. a talisman. a sure sign.

i have a habit of tucking common signs and wonders into
my pockets. i carry them home with me. late at night i hold
them up to my ear and listen to the sounds they make.

perhaps you do this too?

i walked empty in search of a miracle, but the iris was kind
enough to show herself just above the boggy green of the
pond and there was just enough strapping leaf for my eyes
to hold onto.

it was all i could do to stop myself from climbing out of the
boat and walking onto the water. it has been done before.

but i was afraid that i would sink like a stone and silently go under, the waves just waiting to drag me down and swallow me whole.

i was afraid there would be no voice to calm the storm. there are entire seasons in which i carry my faith in a teaspoon.

still, there was the leaf. there was the iris.

and everywhere i looked there were things bursting into life. drops of yellow were scattered over the small blades of gorse and the smell of it was a reliable thing.

have you ever smelled gorse on a sunny day? it was a small consolation calling my name across the withered reeds and the dead grasses.

there are lives that you have not tasted.
you should be glad for this. i am.

i know the outline of mine well by now. each selvedge is familiar. i know most of my wants and desires by name.
i have long conversations with my aching losses.

of course, you have hidden lives too—the names of which i have not been introduced to.

there are corners that i probably would not want to inhabit.
i fear that i might not be strong enough.

i want to hear your stories and i want to tell mine.

there are days that my life reminds me that i am only just remembering how to breathe.

a body can forget how to exhale.

i have done this, and yet, somehow i have survived.

some things need to be learnt from the beginning. from scratch. a lesson in how to let go of the air inside your lungs. i have struggled with this.

there have been times that i have forgotten the shape of hope, its quiet voice, and always breathing just beneath the unmarked surface of my skin, there lies shame, holding my mute tongue in its crippled hands.

i so often yield my life to its toothless presence.
when i have allowed myself to be held hostage by it, i end up robbing you.

all the honest moments in which you could have said to yourself in your most relieved voice, the one you fetch from the cupboard when another tired body has stripped themselves of their outside skin in front of you:

dear God, thank you. this is me too.

what i mean to say, is that i am not here to tell you
how to live your life. all your stories belong to you.

i am only here to tell about mine. there are corners of it that you would not want to live in.

we forget the things that call us to each other, the courage of the telling.

how we all need water. how we hold cups with which we might serve each other.

we need to hear failure fall from each other's mouths. shame withers in the presence of this, and then having been seen, an ordinary miracle occurs—we unfurl.

we begin to live.

dear God, thank you. this is me too.

i am not here to tell you how to live your life.
i am here to tell about mine.

this is what i am trying to say with this poem.

the invitation

outside my bedroom window, in a slice of porcelain sky
a small flock of starlings mount the wind
each pulsing body sleek and sure
they are wing and instinct
cutting the air into wide strips of joy
and i
soft, domesticated animal that i am, witness
from behind double layers of thick glass
the invitation.

things to tell yourself when it all falls apart

when they start to growl and bare their thorny teeth
—all the obedient words you have always chosen
to describe your life, you might decide in that first
raw moment, to wrap yourself up in hope, swaddle
the small, tender things
that you have told yourself will live—*must* live, because
you need it to be so.
because without them your life would surely come apart
at the seams. split irreparably. irredeemably.

perhaps this is the thing that you fear. the falling apart.

a life can be repaired, you know.

you might sing them a lullaby. placate them
with your own body.
you might make up your own words for this
—new words.
in the chaos you might even call it *faith.*

still, tomorrow has not yet drawn its first breath.
the things that live in that unpromised place will not be
renamed for anything that they are not.
not yet.

there are things that will never be yours—to eat this, and
live through it, is to inhabit your life just as it is.

a certain courage.

you might choose to open your hands, to let things go.
you might allow a new story to shape itself if it wants to.

everything that ends is the birth of a new story.
this is all you have. this is all that you are given.
the soft yielding to what you do not know.
not yet.

already it exists. somewhere to the left of you it waits.

perhaps, this is the thing you fear even more. *surrendering.*

a life can be repaired, you know.

be even more beautiful than it once was. it can.
it has been done before.

nothing is beyond the reach of beauty. and grace.

when it starts to crack, starts to fall apart without your
permission—tell yourself this.

picking the rubble for signs of light

perhaps, it is time to start picking through the rubble for all that remains. you might begin to shape a new thing out of the fragments. a new life.
you will learn to love this one too.
you will teach yourself how.
but listen, do not make something for the bodies who are watching your life, waiting to drape their opinions around your neck.
what if this were your last year? what would you look for?
who would you choose to share a breathing space with?
where would you plant your eyes and your attention?
you need a reason to unfold your sleep-soft body from the battlefield of the night, still hungering for rest, and then choose to live one more day.
sometimes, being alive is hard work. it is all so fragile.
no one else knows how you have to part the curtain to the ordinary, each new day, searching for portions of beauty to sustain you.
how there are days when the searching in corners, and under the sofa, and behind the secrets of the bookshelf, leads to nothing but dust.
there are moments when i stand still on my bare feet and eat gratitude for the cut-glass prism that hangs in front of my window—how it catches the light from outside, throwing rainbows all over the places that i still know how to find.
beauty is a series of waypoints dotted along the spine of my life. it is the antidote to many things, but mostly sadness and its larger, looming cousin—despair.
i have made a life out of searching for beauty, and searching

for beauty, has made me who i am.
i am trying to show you something that is growing on the back of my own life.
sometimes, we lose track of what we once held as lodestar.
the waypoints disappear, or worse, no longer hold meaning.
when this happens you only have a handful of choices.
you might refuse to move, choose to stay in the same place suspended in a web of confusion. the safety of this is at once satisfying, and numbing.
or you might try and find your way back to the last place that felt safe and familiar.
this requires a *walking back*. a return.
think carefully about this. some of us are so afraid of the unknown, that we will eat anything given to us and call it a feast. failure often hides in the long grass here.
or you might get up onto your knees and move in any direction. throw the dice, trusting that a new path will open as you force your body through the unfamiliar landscape.
remember that you are both the compass and the map.
careful though, because others leave their marks on your surface as well. be wise about whose markings you use as waypoints, especially if you have no head for direction.
i know the taste of this too.
but also, allow me to give you this: clearings await.
they are out there.
i know this. i have found my way to them before.
if you cannot see them yet, just keep moving.
if it is all that you can do, then crawl.
don't be dismayed at the speed of your pace.
rest when your knees can't take the pain anymore.
i know what despair feels like. fear too.
they both know my name.

there, i have said it. i have let it escape from my mouth.
but i also know how to unpick their burrs from my skin.
i am relentless at this.
i have no other choice.
i pick them like overripe fruit, then leave them all over the house, so that the light might find them—might allow them to soften. to rot. to disintegrate.
sometimes, i go back and pick them up again.
there, i have said it. i have let it escape from my mouth.
i am a life shaped by thousands of singular moments, and yet i couldn't name each one if i tried.
but they are real. they exist. they happened.

here's the thing:

everything that once satisfied you, doesn't anymore, because there are new places for you to discover, both inside your own existence, as well as outside your own comfort.
new courage doesn't grow on trees, you know.
it grows in the raw places where you have picked at your fear.
courage is the scab that covers the small wound.
the scar is the proof that you fought and lived.
do not underestimate the magnitude of this.
beauty often hides under rocks and there is no place that the light can't get to.
if you are reading this from the rubble of your life, perhaps it is time to start searching for the fragments that remain.
you might begin to shape a new thing. a new life.

in time, you will learn to sit comfortably with it.
in time, you might even fall completely in love with it.
in time, you will wonder how you ever wanted anything else.

a bonfire of failures

what if you kept it safe
a small, burning coal in the hollow of your chest

you might let it burn
let others warm their hands on everything
you think is failure

your life is not as small as you think it is

look again

it isn't the size of the darkness that matters.

i think this is enough

i would like to give you a talisman to hold onto
—a small solace for when you are afraid.

something soft and downy. a thing that does not ask
for anything. a thing that only knows how to be *presence.*
a rare thing, like silky hair on the back of a new-born's
head. how each strand remember the weight of the hands
that spun them out of nothing. for a while at least, they still
know the tenderness of it. the great wonder.
—God, if you believe, otherwise you might want to call it a
miracle. a beautiful thing. a gossamer co-incidence.

it does not matter.

when you are not looking, they all answer to the same
name anyway.

perhaps, i might give you this:

the moonlight finding me last night.
the milky pools spilling all over the windowsill.
the country of my skin soaking it up like water.

the memory of it remains clear. how we yearn to be found.
i cannot name this. perhaps you already understand?

if you can see my words behind your eyes, then
set them free inside that vast, hidden room to which you
escape. that rich, inner place where you are free.

once there, take it from my hands—this small thing.
how it fits the waiting nest of the palm, the curve of
your hand as it moves at once to make a fist.

bracing itself, preparing for impact, but instead, finding
ribbons of light trailing all the way from sun to moon.

hope reflected. a pure thing.

perhaps, the purest.

how there is always enough light to wake us up, to rouse us
from the hundred-year sleep that numbs—to stir us
onward, and onward, and onward as the light moves.

our eyes always searching for the flicker of it in the dark.

our soft bodies always straining to find our way home.

felicity

this is not for every tender body that walks into my words today, but it is for some soft body, somewhere.

and you will know very soon whether it fits the shape of the hollow inside your chest. wait for it.

come, sit here at my kitchen table. just move the books and the embroidery thread. there you go. here, let me pour you a cup of tea. tell me, how is your heart?

does it still know how to pluck the feathers from the naked body of despair? does it weep often? when you woke up this morning was *hope,* a small, dead bird, already cold inside your mouth?

did you also pull yourself from shallow pools of sleep, with thin threads of courage, to keep someone you love, alive?

and there are so many ways in which we are lifeboats, whilst trying to swim the ocean with a feeble breaststroke.

they say that most people drown silently.
no screams, or cries for help.
perhaps, they think they are still doing ok, until it is too late to fight the undercurrent.

tell me, do you also look at what everyone else is doing?

do you pin your eyes to everything that they are achieving?

what about the ache inside of you when you witness how easily they push themselves into the empty spaces that you have longed to inhabit. i know.

all the dreams you once had, now mute ghosts in the locker.

and there are so many things that demand your seconds, and your minutes, and your hours.

and you are tired, and tired, and tired. i know.

all the sapling dreams that you plant, withering for lack of attention, and light, and water.

and you are caught—suspended, within the things that you want to say, and write, and make.

the sharp outline of the life that you once wanted, calls to you plaintively. how to marry it to the shape of your days.

all the things that you want to send out into the world, but also, at your hip, there are all the soft bodies who need you. the soft bodies who depend on you for water, and food, and clean clothes, and how to say the word, *dream.* and they need vitamins, and apples, and you are fresh bread, baked daily.

and, *for-what-they-are-about-to-receive-are-they-truly-thankful?*

and they need to be hugged, and loved, and held close. and they need freedom to run, but also, they need to be kept safe.

how is one body expected to know all the answers to this?

and they need to be taken to playdates, because they say that *play* is the work of childhood but see how we forget to dish it up for ourselves.

there is so much that escapes us when we forget how to look for joy.

and they need swimming lessons for fun, but also for in case they fall into an unfriendly body of water whilst your eyes are away eating flowers, or moss, or dangerously nibbling at the shape of a large cloud in the middle of the day.

still, you are a lifeboat, even when you are away from them.

also, a lighthouse. a shelter.
you are all these things.

and once-upon-a-time you still thought that you could be everything for everyone—meet all the needs and demands that called your name. how you believed that you could stretch yourself, rubbery, from one body to another and still find your way home to your own inner country—that once familiar place that threads itself through the dreams that you have held safely wrapped in puffs of cotton wool since you were young. i know.

may i tell you something that i am learning at night?
may i share the wisdom that finds me when i am lost in a forest of questions in the dark hours?

there is nothing in your life that is more important than the bodies that you have been planted with. this is a truth.

none of your work, nothing that you might create, is more important than breathing a kind life into a small body, or into a sick body, or into a *body-that-your-body-knows-so-well,* but now their body has forgotten yours—forgotten their own name, and you have become mother, or father, no longer the lover, and this is a grief shaped liked loss, but you do it.

you travel this new country, map-less and brave, because you *are* love. already this is a tender work of art.

how you heap grace onto empty plates, every minute of the day, so that their bodies will be filled, and filled, and filled.

how you are building generous boundary lines inside of them with your presence, with your love.

this is the planting of a forest.
this is the *lifting of your eyes up to the mountain.*
this is the *wondering from which direction your help might come from.*

all your losses have names, and they follow you.

and a long time ago, a man once said that even mountains could throw themselves into the sea, and even then, people were left confused and aching.
and still even now. i know.

perhaps, what he *meant,* was that mountains crumble slowly. sometimes they need to be carried away pebble by pebble. this is the miracle.

the throwing is slow, hard work. determined work.

the kind of *throwing-into-the-water* that only happens in its own time. and time will not be told what to do.

and you might be told that what you do is unimportant.
you might also be told that *who* you are is unimportant, or rather, *who-you-are-not*, and you must pay attention to this, to their words, but also *not.*
some words are for eating. others are for spitting out.
even better to not taste them at all.

there are always voices telling you *what* to believe.
do not believe all of them.

they will tell you about the *things-that-need-to-be-done* for you to feel fulfilled, and some of these are important, i know, so please do not misunderstand me.

what i am trying to say, is this:

you are a secret life of veils, and needs, and hidden things.

but also, the world is hurting and there is tender work to be done, but you cannot do it all because your life will crumble under the weight of it, or perhaps grow sour like old milk.

nothing is more important than the soft bodies with which you are planted. nothing. nothing. nothing.

almost everything has been done before and will probably be done again. *there is nothing new under the sun.*
even right now, someone out there is doing exactly what you want to do, and maybe they are even *taking* from you and

quietly shaping it into their own. this hurts. it rips at your confidence. it steals the hope.

but know this too—they can never take what you are made of, because you are a presence unlike any other, and you have a voice that nobody else could ever speak with. rest in this. if they take what is yours without asking, and boldly carve their own name on it, they will spend their days searching for their own voice deep within the lives of others.
what they need to do is come home to themselves.

and we have all been lost and searching, knocking on doors.

we are all making a life in a season different to that of others.

if you were to step off the earth today, straight into the next cloud-room, having only made the world a gentler place for one other body, then already you have done holy work.

already you have done enough. tell yourself this.

and you might worry about how you will feed the mouths of the soft bodies who grow around you. and you might spend more time awake than you do sleeping, for fear of losing the hours in which to shape something that might be exchanged for a few small coins, but also know this:

worry eats too, and it is never satisfied, and fear is a voice that shouts, stilling all the others. somehow it all works out. good things have found me, and they will find you too. just trust.

this is not for every tender body that walks into my words

today, but tell me—did it fit the shape of the hollow inside
your chest?

your life is a season long and seasons are always changing.

don't get caught on the thorns.
plant your mustard seeds. your flowers. your apple trees.
allow them to take root.

if you listen for them, you will hear their faithful promises.

already the *waiting*, is a rich and fertile place.

the day you say your own name with love

it will taste so much better
than anything another body could give you
—when you find your way home to your own skin.
when in fresh delight
you turn to your own life, wrapping yourself
tightly around your own frame.
there will be no threat of leaving, no wandering
enthrallment.
here you will see the empty cup. the half-full plate. you will
know presence from promise, or at least
you will begin to taste it, knowing that it soured a while ago
—was thin to begin with, and it will hurt.
but listen, it is entirely possible to wake up one morning
holding the word *enough,* in your mouth.
when this happens, you must pay attention.
something is waiting for your permission, for your *no*
and for your *yes.*
—there are no *maybes* here.
you might not know this yet, but this is a small sacrament.
a little miracle. a fresh birth.

blessed be

i have breakfast with God every morning
long after they tell me i pronounce his name wrong
that he won't come if i call him—me
with my soft breasts full of rebellion, my ways
that remind them of witchcraft, all the wisdom
of the grandmothers
when i pass him the cinnamon
i ask: *tell me, am i made in your image, or not?*
to which he laughs, lifts up his shirt
shows me how he is shaped like a mountain
the curve of his chest is Loch Fyne
teeming with life
in his hair i find strands of oak moss
wolf lichen grows from his fingernails
the air in my kitchen is thick and hoary
salty with things that i do not want to forget
after he leaves i will have to sweep up the heather
that falls where he sits
i keep the flowers on the table next to my pencil
and the paper on which i write all the ways
in which i am loved
when i ask after his health, whether his womb
has also stopped working
he smiles
as only another woman who no longer has need of a
calendar, might
when he asks for something to drink, i give him water
drawn from the well inside my mouth
i tell him that i am grateful for the year of my birth

the safety of it, knowing full well that i am afraid of fire
of flames licking at my skirt, of being thrown in the ice
of a river in winter, sink and your name is pure
float, and you are dead
in the name of all that is holy
long after he tells me they pronounce his name wrong
God still knocks on my door, still visits
we have breakfast together every morning
he tells me there is no sweeter water than that
which i give him to drink.

tender weapons that dwell inside the mouth

when the world tries to force its way in
through the cage of your bones, just to make trouble
just to see what you might shape with the soft trowel
that is your tongue, you must remember that you are water

a thousand invocations inhabit the womb of your mouth
and thousands more, if you use them well

everything is a seed, everything waits to give birth
to something

beneath the wet blanket of your tongue
there is always *life*, but *death* stands with ears pricked
waiting for his turn, waiting to leave behind
that fertile valley

you must remind yourself of where you live, you must
choose for yourself what you will do

what you will give

even today, i have sharpened the wrong sword, used
the wrong weapon, drawing blood with my words
when what i really wanted was to plant kindness

to wield a ploughshare
to harvest peace.

a story of the waters that hold me

i want to tell you a story about water. a story about the thirsty moments in which i must force myself to slow down, and the thin moments in which i allow myself to occupy only the smallest corner of mother earth's generous skin.
there are days on which my life is a long pause and i walk the thin slivers between here and there, with my feet bare. it is a quiet rebellion against the noise-making machine of this world which i inhabit.
within this liminal space, i remember the presence of almost each body of water that i have ever been immersed in.
there have been many. water has always held me.
here are the fun-filled, chlorine-laced swimming pools of my childhood, and memories of playing *Marco Polo* on hot days with my brothers. our young bodies still oblivious to all the different names of *grief* that we would still have to learn.
and all the salty oceans engraved with hungry riptides.
waves dotted with the sleek, wetsuit-clad bodies of surfers.
there are winding, willing streams of mountain water veining through the dust-in-the-mouth landscape where i first felt a sense of geographical grief, after my unwilling roots were ripped up when we had to relocate to a large city.
the loss of my near-feral childhood has left me searching for the chimera of stability my entire life.
i have still not found it. this *searching*, is the warp and the weft of every story that eventually leaves my body in search of its own independent life.
and there, right at the back of a room inside my head, is the stage-sunken pool filled with the captured, indoor water in which i was baptised; rushed into like a lost sheep.

i was still carrying the weight of an angry God, given to me by others.
there were so many questions that i swallowed whole with my tight throat.
there are many things that i regret, but i do not regret loving God. now, with my silvering presence i no longer swallow things that should be said aloud, and i am no longer a part of any fold that doesn't love with its arms wide open.
the courage to leave that familiar security behind came from somewhere deep within.
i do not know its source, but it tastes like peace.
still, there are things that i miss and there are things that i am missing from.
now, i am an outsider by choice, almost a crone. a planter of provocative questions. a willing outlier. a quiet rebel.
and even right now, as i am preparing to follow the way that this story is trying to take me on, i am sitting in an unfamiliar bath, in an unfamiliar cottage, in water fragrant with rose geranium oil lapping at my grateful thighs.
there are many more fluid places pooling secretly within the vessel that is my life. i remember them. water has always held me. for a body who was born under the stubborn solidity of an earth sign, i am mysteriously drawn to water, or rather, i am swallowed whole by the cohesiveness of it. how droplets hold onto each other, and hold onto each other, and hold onto each other, until they are forced apart.
i am a body of molecules drawn to an analogous kin.
the body does not forget.
my cells remember their watery birth, perhaps even further back than the womb. they have the wrinkled memories of the grandmother of the ancient-of-days.
but one must be careful where one says these things aloud.

between the pages of this book seems a safe enough place.
still, someone will read this and find that the inside of their chest will burn with a slow and fierce anger.
they will tell themselves that it is a righteous anger, that they feel called to defend God.
i do not mind this. i do not write to offend.
i write only to tell my own truth. my own stories.
God is always present, weaved into the fabric of my being.
perhaps, now you might see why i travel the perimeter of my life on light feet?
the world that i once inhabited, the voices that i once allowed to tell me who i am and how i am allowed to fit in, have no time for women who are stitched together with the scarlet thread of uncomfortable questions.
questions that are never allowed to be asked aloud.
i am all these things. and i am also silvery fish, and ancient song-singing whale, unapologetically barnacled with failures.
there have been so many. it doesn't do to look away.
but i have grown redolent with the pungent scent of courage.
i am fat with favour and rich with grace.
everything that i am and everything that i am not, is all grace.
i am a body that needs to keep moving, a body that needs to keep touching, a body that was given ravenous eyes that hunger to *see* everything around me.
i need to eat colour, and texture, and shape.
i can conjure up the earthy smell of the icy mountain water leaving the deep stone-womb of the Tsitsikamma forest and the warm waves of the Indian ocean riffling towards the beach at Port Alfred. the tidal pool at Kalk Bay waits for me to tell you of all her wonders and how the cold Atlantic feeds her. these are the waters of the continent that birthed me. Africa, with her stories, and heartache, and resilient people.

and here? what about this place that now holds the roots of my life. the roots of my ancestors. Scotland. even now, even as i shape these words, the green waters of the Sound of Jura sing their mysterious songs to the ancient moisture seeping through the rocks.
rocks that are fragrant and lusty with heathery things that grow largely undisturbed, but for the presence of the wind claiming the flora on their lichened stone beds. how it shapes the stems and the leaves into a home for the breathing things that need a warm, yielding roof over their pulsing bodies. everything is held, even within the wildness.
did you know that water can be the same loamy shades as lichen, or moss, or soil? as a child i used to wear down all the blue crayons in the box with pages, and pages of drawings of raindrops, and curly-waved azure oceans. i love blue.
but what is blue? blue is the body of the sky on *some* of her days, but not all of them. blue is five-petalled forget-me-nots with their yellow hearts, covering the feet of gravestones in forgotten graveyards. blue is the cobalt sea-glass that i covet. the smooth promise of it amongst the wet rocks.
if i give you a piece of blue sea-glass, you should know that you quietly and persistently inhabit a corner of my heart.
water isn't really blue. we are told that it is. for a while we believe it too, but there are many things that aren't what we think they are.
as for me, the story goes that i took my own time to arrive in this world. for five long days i travelled that short, sacred journey from womb to air, finally drawing breath with my new lungs just as the dawn arrived on a crisp autumn morning. it seems i was unwilling to leave the safety of my mother's amniotic fluid, the quiet embrace of it. perhaps a prescience left behind in my bones was particularly strong.

perhaps, a visceral imprint, a certain knowing that somehow water would always hold me weightless; that it would always be a place of *floating without judgement.* the clamorous mouth of the world muted. the body remembers.
there are days on which we reluctantly take what we are given and then we learn how to make new things from it. we decide to do this. *choice,* is both a sword and a ploughshare.
at first, we accept them, these unwanted gifts, so that later we might lick them with our strong, unwilling tongues.
we take them into our protesting mouths and eat them.
we tell ourselves that they taste good. that they are pleasant.
that we are no longer hungry for what we once wanted.
for what we have just received make us truly thankful and help us to forget what we have been given. help us to forget what we really wanted.
the lies we tell ourselves in order to survive.
do you know this too?
we think that we believe our own words, but our bodies are listening, always eavesdropping inside the microscopic pools of each cell, always aware of each lacuna filled with lack.
with our eyes cast up to the mountain in plastic gratitude, we mourn everything that we have told ourselves we don't really want. all the lies that become a second mouth.
the voices of the unlived lives of our mother, or our father.
we secretly long for the freedom, or in my case, the life that i longed to carve onto my bones if the punishment wasn't loss, or exile. if i were to close my ears to the *second names* of the god that are still being forced onto me in love and great kindness, i would tell you the way to each holy well in which i have swam—the shallow waters into which i have willingly waded, my skin alert to the presence of trouble that always follows any mammal who dares to leave the herd.
how the shallows turned into *deep-calls-to-deep*, all the shallows

where i would begin to forget the smell of the holy buildings i was forced to sit in. all the churches that i was given. all the tests i had to pass in order to prove that i knew the things that God has actually hidden from me.
all the tender acceptance that was kept from the softness of my being by self-appointed gatekeepers and scribes. all the rules they called *freedom,* and all the laws, and the strangling ropes of red tape.
there are so many things that make them angry.
the sins of my father, and his father, and the fathers without a name.
all the loud sins, and the quiet ones, even the secret ones— the ones that were never owned up to by the actual sinner.
all mine to carry and watch over until they could be handed over to the milky body of my baby son.
but never mind any of this if you do not have breasts, or wilful desires, and are not consumed by unvoiced rebellion.
where the words in the holy books, and the words in the holy man-shaped mouthpieces said that i had no choice but to reap what i hadn't sown, even the things done behind closed doors by other hands.
some were given unto me.
others were just left outside the back door for me to find.
what does a soft heart, a curious heart, a feral heart, do with a weaponised God?
i chose to walk away.
rather the desert than a poisoned well.
there are many things that aren't what we think they are.
i have seen this. it is all a part of the stories that live inside my hair and that breathe through my skin.
i am water, but i am also the first miracle, with the names of a new God, hidden safely inside every cell of my body.

i won't tell you what these names are, because there are some things that we need to find out for ourselves.
if you want me to, i might show you the sweeping curves of the inner landscape in which i dwell.
i might show you the valleys that i have walked and the plains that i hope to never return to. how they nearly destroyed me.
but only if you really want to know, because there are many hearts tired of having things forced upon them.
you might want to drink from the water that flows through my stories and if you find the sweetness that they hold, you might see how there are many things that *are,* what we think they are *not.*
we all have names for the places we call home.
my stories are about a body being lost, a soft body who was once called, *shame.*
how i still fight that name.
how i am found, over, and over, and over.
how the getting lost still happens a hundred times a day.
how the getting *found* is not about returning to the camp with shame stuck in my mouth, but about a God who lets me run because there is love, and love, and love.
and how this love is the real thing.
how this love is truly *unconditional.* i know this fiercely.
my stories are about walking away, and about being true to the quiet voice that sits on the ledge of the heart, or on the edge of a bridge.
right on the edge.
my stories are water, and water, and water.
they seek thirst. these are the things that live inside of me.
the tender things that i choose to set free into the world.
all the watery light that calls me home. perhaps you know this too? travel gently friend. i'll see you on the road.

you might want to read this as a blessing

if you wanted to, you could live right here, exactly where you are, knowing that your feet are planted right on the edge of this ocean, or perhaps the silent womb of a loch filled with germinal secrets.
and if you wanted to, you could dwell here forever.
build your altar. shape it out of small stones, so that you can take it apart whenever you need to.
and you *will* need to, because grace will find you on her gentle feet, to prove you wrong. over, and over.
this is a quiet declaration. a sure thing.
wisdom knows when to dismantle her own holy altars.
build a fire. all wandering bodies need a place to warm their hands. keep it banked. make it a safe place for any breathing being, but especially for the breathing bodies of all your enemies. and whilst you are shaping a forgiving shelter with your life, pray that on the far side of the water your enemies are doing the same thing, because grace will look for you on her gentle feet, to prove you wrong. over, and over.
this is a quiet declaration. a sure thing.
put up your tent. ask your God to enlarge it if you think you need more than what you have already been given. but think carefully about what you ask for, about what you *think* you need, because sometimes *more* is really *less.*
again, this is a small truth that can breathe on its own.
already there is the light that finds you each morning.
there is the promise of new heather rippling purple on the soft sage of the fells. here is the hum of the bees and the stars of your ancestors swept up every night in that inky blanket. just look up. they will never leave you. you are never

far from anybody who has ever loved you. all their stardust and all their atoms have left their imprint on you—their mark. and afterwards, you will be returned to those who are still to follow. they are waiting on the edges. dwelling unseen on the fringes of that other place.
and on that day, your name will be *ancestor.*
how holy is this!
but for now, you have this—your breath, and the tenacious thrum of blood against the walls of each meticulous vein.
the tensile strength of each ligament and bone in your frame.
the faithfulness of the hyoid bone anchoring the muscles of your throat. always holding things up. the way in which the delicate arch of it allows you to swallow the goodness of the earth, allows you to praise the gladdening beauty, allows you to speak the unbinding of all that shackles. how your body is a conduit. how you are a collection of impulses.
and here you are just wandering your life so unaware until things are removed from you.
pay attention. listen to all the ways in which you might want to say *yes,* and *no,* and *enough.*
always consider what it is to which you are speaking.
do not underestimate the worth of this freedom, the cost that others have paid on your behalf without knowing your name. without knowing the intimate details of the fabric of your being. the daily minutiae of your choices. each of your unassuming peculiarities.
the shape of the life that you are weaving on the frame of their sacrifices. all the hidden layers of it.
even your own body, how she is a marvel.
always working towards homeostasis.
always communicating with you in her own quiet way.
please, listen!

you are wonderfully able, whenever you want, to send your eyes out exploring to any new place, to wade out towards the wet horizon. think of this, or at least reach out your hand to it. it will respond to your courage. to your trust.
small prophecies will find you.
you will know them by the way that your body will exhale at the sound of their voices, their bird-like songs that will cut through the layers of noise like a silver bell.
in front of you is the mouth of an ocean. hold the vastness of this body of water in front of everything that you have stumbled through. water knows no failure.
perhaps this holds a lesson for you?
there are no failures here.
only a collection of dovetailed moments that you have lived through, that you have *experienced* your way through.
you are not a failure.
you are not a mistake.
you are not a thing called, *shame.*
you are not unlovable.
you are unfinished wisdom still learning your own name.
you have not arrived, and you never will.
i do not yet know what happens in that other room that we step into when we encounter that mysterious thinning—that waiting moment when each of us walks through the liminal space.
i only know that i am keeping my being open to love, and to great kindness, and to compassion.
and grace.
this is enough for me.
remind your body that you were made to swim, that you come from water, that you still *are* water.
you are an explorer. you have not been given a map.

you are the map-writer. the way-shower. show your eyes the horizon and your feet the soft sand. use what you have been given. all of it. wring it out and ask for more.
once you have thrown the dry bones on the table in front of you, you might begin to sing.
you might begin to use your thighs as a drum, a calling card for beauty. for purpose.
use all the words that live inside your mouth.
speak what you want to see.
call it by its name. call it to your life.
give it a place to take root. you have been given this!
you have the authority.
say, *please* and *thank you.*
remind yourself daily in your own tongue—the dialect that tastes like truth, that your compass points towards home.
already this is a collection of promises. believe them.
already you are rich. believe this too, although it might feel fragile in your hands.
it is a sure thing. a quiet declaration. a tender weapon.
use it well.

everywhere and in everything

i have already stumbled across God several times today.
all the ways in which i have prayed, and none of them
needing words.

licking the bones of a common gospel

i talk with God about dangerous things—for the ways to open up before me, as well as within me. i have been stitched together out of hand-me-down stories and i have a hard time standing up under the weight of some memories. i have made a habit out of keeping doors locked and keeping my bones away from the light. it is what it is.
we have known each other from before i was born, God and i—from long before i had the name that i was given for this short moment in time, and from before i had the soft thighs that i now do hard battle with every day and because of this we sit in the mornings and drink tea together, God and i—me, drinking from my favourite cup and saucer, the one with an old story that i do not know, but which i am now a part of, and God with a wineskin of vinegar. i unpack all the things that eat at my peace, and i say: *here, you can have it! i don't know what to do with all this fear. please make it go away. please remind me what hope tastes like, because i am beginning to forget.* and then God smiles at me in the same way that i smile at the boy who grew within me for forty weeks, and for whom i would give my life in an instant, and really, there is nothing more that i need to know. this is enough.
and afterwards, we talk about the soft rain, and the blackbird in the tree across the road, and the way that love tastes different to each mouth and having read this common gospel that is shaped like the inside of all my hidden lives—having licked its bones clean for the hunger within me, i get up from my bed, and *live.*

shaping the quiet prophecy of a life

if you believe that you are water
and you are
stop trying to fit into another body's small cup
you are bigger than this, and wilder
—feral, if you would only allow yourself to remember
within your body there is thirsty ground to cover, and trees
waiting to be watered
the old oak and the new sycamore, the dogwood
and the goat willow
are waiting for you to bless them, waiting
for you to green them
here are the darting, glittery fish
who long to swim in the estuaries of your life
and the soft bodies of sleek mammals
slipping unseen through your quiet, ferrying
your stories on their wet fur, all the things
that you believe about yourself, and all the things
that you have been given
they might secretly long to bring you something true
an offering to drop at your feet
you might let them tell you
that you are not a mouthful, that you are not
a moment to be captured, held in a bowl
you are the rain waiting to be reborn
you are cloud, and the soft lapping at the edge of the reeds
you are the unwitnessed wave at play in the ocean
a womb is made to hold, as well as to let go

if you allow your body this, you might begin to wear
all your days pinned to your breast pocket
where you can reach them with your untroubled hands
kiss them with your satisfied mouth—an honest place
this is a small truth.

believe this.

you are a thousand other stories too

i don't really want to talk about it anymore—
the thing that has grown accustomed to my name.
ivy, snaking up my walls. its sticky mouth holding on.
refusing to make space for other things. how i water it
every week, give it light and a place in which to breathe.

how i say:

this is all mine.
this is what was done to me.
this is what i have been given.
i vow to keep it alive, to keep taking cuttings to plant in little pots.
in case i begin to forget the sharpness of it, the bitter taste.

but lately, things are starting to silver themselves all over
me. even my words shy away when i call them.
they have always been too honest.

they say: *oh no, not this again.*
they say: *it is time, let it go now.*
they say: *you are a thousand other stories, not just one.*

rip it off the stone. show it just enough mercy to keep
yourself from returning to check its pulse, just enough
mercy to dispose of its body.

let's tie it up with an old rope. attach it to a new rock.
let's drop it over the edge. watch it sink.
once and for all, let's leave it behind.

see how it is November again. pay attention to the light.

you are circling closer to the door, closer to the moment
in which you will have just enough time to say:

wait. so soon? is it already time to go?

in which you will say:

wait.
is this really what mattered the most?
is this what i held onto?

stop! please. i am not ready yet.

i only want to remember the things i should have held closer.
i only want to remember the things i should have loved better.

even right now there is the light

here are the soft-sage waters of the loch
and the stones that have known the quiet of her belly.
my hands cannot tell if they belong, or if they yearn for the
deep—whether they long to return.

in the naked sky, a gull cuts the air with his soft feathers.
he does not care that he is being watched. oblivious
to my tender spots, or how the fear that sleeps with me
at night, climbs onto my back each morning.
even right now
it is here, reminding me of what it likes to eat.
it never strays far from the paper walls that i erect, flames
issuing from its nostrils and me, always trying
to be water. always trying to look away
from its apocalyptic face. to turn
from its noxious presence.

there are worlds, upon worlds, existing parallel to ours.
we think that we are alone. we think
that we are the only ones.
even right now
the gull only knows how to be what he has been
given—a crisp, brief life that owes nobody anything.
he undresses this as his life's work.
i wonder if he misses things.
things that were taken from him. ask me how i know this.

all around me hundreds of unbodied tragedies
are unfolding.

even right now, as you read this, in this moment, and *this*
one, and again right now, somewhere in some unfamiliar
shadowland, a stranger is begging for something precious.
to hold onto it for just a little while longer.

they will not be given it. ask me how i know this.

instead, they will have to learn how to keep breathing
on the blade of its absence, how to keep on existing
even right now, as you read this, in *this moment*, and *this*
one, and again, and again.

even when their knees have calloused over, and they
have forgotten how to hold up their hands
in surrender, instead, preferring to look away.
choosing to avert their hungry gaze.

they will have to learn how to undress *loss,* as their life's
work. ask me how i know this.

here is the afternoon light, falling at my feet.
the way that it collapses onto the rocks.
the way that it does not resist.
how it melts into the beach.
softens what is heavy.

even when i don't look for it, even when i absolutely
refuse to beg for it, it still finds me.

even right now, there is the light.
ask me how i know this.

all your waters have washed over me and i live

deep calls to my deep.
into your wide peace i go.
where you are, i rest.

a story of storms and water

outside, beyond the thick, white walls of the cottage a storm is growing herself bigger across the waters.
angry skies, roiling with slate-tipped warheads of water, are waiting impatiently to make love to the turbulent, restive waves whipping themselves across the Sound of Jura.
in front of the fire i am a woman crouched low.
with my oldest eyes i watch and wait as things unfold.
not the things outside, no—storms take care of themselves.
i am not afraid of the outside storm. i have seen enough to know that they pay no heed to human intervention.
the storms that need to be honoured with a deep, sacred bow, are the ones that build for themselves a chapel within the boundaries of a life. when they arrive, they can only be observed with kindness and grace.
they must be left to do their work—the washing away, the uncovering, the clearing of the stale air.
i am marking this germinal moment with an apprehensive curiosity and a nod to my inner tempest. my familiar squall.
she is all grown up now, but she still has the heart of a child.
she wants to carve a life for herself outside of the small rooms within which i keep her safe.
she refuses to be owned by anyone.
she has marked me in her resistance to bow the knee.
what i mean to say with these words is that i am waiting for a harvest of courage to bloom within my bones. there are things that need to be told and there are stories that want to be heard. entire sentences desire to live outside my mouth.
they have held me hostage for too long.
does that sound strange?

that i am both hostage and keeper? anyone with a life tied to others, and really isn't that all of us, will know precisely what i mean.
and these stories? i am still not entirely sure what they want. perhaps, to show the way, or to be a small light.
maybe they just want to create chaos—to run down the road with their canteen voices, singing and shouting at the top of their unholy lungs. holy mountains of threadbare loincloths discarded everywhere. prayer flags to the earth.
perhaps they just want to exist outside of something.
outside of *me.*
i am not all that i am cracked up to be.
they should *want* to escape me.
isn't this at once a familiar desire?
we all secretly yearn to be seen, no, more than this—to be accepted, despite the cracks in the façade that we try so hard to hide. to have the opportunity to undress all our stories in front of others. to shake off the oilskin that covers us.
to simply be a collection of naked stories.
this requires a *breaking free.*
the leaving of the safety of what is known, for the unknown.
and again, what of these stories that need to escape me?
i want them to feel the cold. i want them to get wet. i want them to scream with the indignity of it all. i want them to eat all the shame that they were shaped out of—to consume their own skin, then lick their lips after the fact.
the process of unbecoming something is seldom lovely, yet there is a fierce beauty that can be found within the struggle.
for a long while i could only witness the process of stripping myself of the layers that were wallpapered onto my being, as a series of failures that answered to *my* name only. even now there are echoes rippling through the ether.

the real work begins after the stories have been allowed to leave. after you have come face-to-face with their truth. you are light and you are darkness. it doesn't do to dress up your darkness as something that it is not. you must know its many names and disarm it with kindness. with acceptance.
then you might begin to heal.
this is a journey of many mountains and many valleys.
there are entire seasons of sitting with my darkness, which have seen me fashion a rope for my own wrists.
i am my own security, as well as my own prison.
it causes me to weep with frustration, and loss, and shame.
still, i am planting a wild garden behind my eyes, despite the storms that i have given cause to happen.
i am ruthless about this.
i don't have enough time left within my days to pat the heads of others who still insist on telling me how i am allowed to spend this one thing that is entirely mine—my life.
a life partly given to me and partly forced upon me.
of course, this is all of us, is it not? we all share this.
every soft body that walks the skin of the earth is given some things as gifts, and force-fed others.
what i am trying to do here, is not for anybody else, although my quest is also for my son.
i do not want him to search for the things that i have lost.
i do not want him to shape his own life in such a way, so that mine might fit me better.
when everything is stripped away, nothing can be taken from you.
this is both terrifying and liberating.
my bare life—the form and the taste of it, will be exposed for everyone to see and they will not have walked any of the valleys with me.

they will be strangers to the nuance of every experience that my body has been through, and i will be at the mercy of this lack of intimate knowledge.
herein lies everything that i fear, and everything that i crave. to be seen for all the things that i am, yes, but also for the things that i am not. not only to be seen, but to be welcomed. no, not only welcomed, but to be *accepted.*
where each of my lived, and unlived lives, are acknowledged. where they are drawn in, sat down, and given a large portion of kindness, and mercy, and grace.
accepted.
this is a much bigger word and far more generous, with wide hips and soft breasts. an ordinary word, with dirt under its fingernails, which has the holy power to undo words that were glued onto me by others. especially the words of the bodies that were supposed to shelter me, but didn't, or couldn't, or perhaps simply refused to.
it is what it is.
i want to live unafraid of my own truth, bearing my own story well—all her softness, as well as her fierceness.
always mindful of the life that was given to me.
i want to be reminded by my own faithful mouth that i have a purpose and a place, although i have had to dig for it with my bare hands. choosing one path takes us from another.
i am respectful of what i have given up.
many of the things that i have walked away from, still speak to me at night. often, all they can do is weep and all i can do is listen. i don't fight it. i let them mourn what they have lost.
i allow loss to write its many names inside my mouth.
allowing grief to be what it is, is a kind thing to do.
a grace.
still, right in the middle of my body, in the very centre of this

body that i call *mine*, there is gratitude. she dwells there, quiet and softly spoken; her hands always held out for more.
she is always respectfully greedy for crumbs, and scraps, and half-eaten portions that others no longer want.
please and *thank you,* grows in my mouth like richly watered moss.
my words are always asking for more because i know that there is more, and i know that things wait to be asked.
they wait to be called. they wait patiently to be invited over.
this is how i wear my faith. i am constantly searching.
i seek and i find.
i seek and i am found.
i stay hungry for more.
there are good things out there. lots of them. and i want to experience them in all their fullness, and so i open my mouth and i call them over, invite them in, and before they have even put on their travelling shoes, i start to prepare a place for them inside the garden behind my eyes.
i say: *thank you for coming!*
i say: *i am waiting for you!*
i say: *look! i have already rearranged the furniture so that you will be comfortable in your new home! you are welcome. you are so welcome!*
there are people who don't like it when you live your life like this, especially if they consider themselves to be holy people.
they want to own misery and hardship, not just live it when it happens in a season. and it does. this is a small truth.
but seasons are seasons, and they are usually short-lived.
but there are people who insist on pitching their tents right outside the doorstep of heaven. and they don't really like things that they cannot control, and life is mysterious, and it is wild and completely uncontrollable, in a raw, feral way.
it is what it is.

i do not want the truth of others to muddy up the waters of my own days.
my life wants more than this.
my life deserves her own voice and so does yours.
admittedly, this sounds simpler than it actually is.
always know whose voice your life is speaking with.
a life is quite capable of being a masterful mimic.
you might have to teach yourself how to do this. it can take half a life, and another half, just to learn how to say *no*.
where your boundaries are thin and diaphanous, it is easy for things to pass in and out through your walls.
an unhealthy osmosis.
then, it is difficult to know where your boundary walls end and where the walls of others begin.
walls are not all bad things.
as long as there are gates to walk through.
as long as you always remember where you keep the keys.
in that fog of enmeshment, you are unable to see how many foreign stories are sewn into the hem of your own coat.
here, i am speaking of the stories that fall from the mouths of the ones we love; the ones we feel duty-bound to rescue.
to find oneself stitched into the fabric of someone else's war can be a difficult thing to escape.
things that can't be escaped are always heavy.
they are burdens that shape a second mouth on the face.
they leave scars on the wrists of our life.
but of course, here on this page, with these words, i have spiralled right back to those ropes. how things that appear to be a safety net, are at times a prison.
then again, all good stories contain a scar, or two.
i have many in my collection, but one day i shall leave them all behind. that elusive, *one day,* which awaits.

that day when i shall step over into the mystery, through the door that leads to the wondrous unknown.
i won't get to take a single thing with me.
nothing is mine.
nothing in this beclouded, ephemeral place is ever ours to own.
some of my stories will remain behind for others to nourish themselves with, so i pay close attention to them.
i pay attention to how i shape my life.
i am not concerned with the stories that others use to shape me, at least not too much.
an untrue word can be undone, although it takes time.
wisdom, is knowing what to let go of.
every day, i rub layers and layers of kindness into my own skin, especially into the dimpled softness of my thighs. there is still a seedbed of hurt tied up in my body. i work at being kindness to myself. it is a sacrament. i know it well.
if i may?
your greatest hurt deserves your greatest kindness.
walk through your life with quiet determination, fully present to the journey—the birdsong, the colour of the sky, the hunger in your belly, the stone stuck between your toes—in other words, embracing the pain, the scars, and the fear, but also, accepting all the shapes of joy. and there are so many.
watch for the way in which the small, breathing moments of delight hold a life together like fine thread.
i am familiar with things that *hold*, and things that bind.
may i give you a small truth?
no other body's life looks like yours.
no other mammal tries to dwell so fog-fisted and so fiercely within the borders of a life, in the same way that you do.
if you have worn your heart down to a fleshy, raw stump

trying to make your days resemble that of another, then you may stop.
is this a relief? i hope that it is. i so often need it myself.
i serve heaping portions of it fresh every day and each time i want to weep with the relief of it.
often, i do not believe myself until long after i have realised that i have lost my appetite for struggling, then i simply yield.
this simple act remains a rebellion.
still, this life?
remember—you don't get to take anything with you, but you do get to leave things behind.
and what you leave behind, are the remains of how much value you placed on being a safe place for other breathing bodies. and when you think about it, there have been many such moments and all of them were opportunities dressed up as quiet warfare.
love is a weapon, you know.
a powerful one.
it is God's favourite weapon of choice.
to love someone when they least deserve it, is to change the fabric of a life. it will always find its way back to you.
no person plants mercy without finding kindness waiting at their own front door.
and what of the small treasures along the way—did you find them? did you pick them up and for a moment, marvel at the wonder of it all?
i have learnt to leave the things that *numb*; the things that fool me into thinking that i have filled up the hunger inside of me.
i don't have to tell you what they are. you have your own tender spots. those thorns that you try so hard to ignore.
you already know their names, although perhaps you still

don't like to say them aloud. you must do this.
it robs them of their power.
you know their names. say them aloud to yourself.
they are thieves. masters of seduction. liars.
all around me, the world with its mouthpiece of opinions, is telling me what to chase after, how to *be*, how to *live my best life*, what to be afraid of, or more truthfully *whom to fear.*
i will not yield to the voices of others who want to force their truth over my head like an ill-fitting sweater.
a child must eat what it is given.
an adult can say *no*, can refuse to take what is forced upon them.
refuse.
it is that simple.
as i write this, i am a woman crouched low.
with my oldest eyes i watch and wait as things unfold inside of me.
tomorrow, the sea will be the same shade of greyish green as the lichen that stubbornly inhabits the walls surrounding the garden.
nature repeats herself everywhere. a series of signs there for those who have eyes to see, and ears to hear.
the waves will do what they are meant to do.
they cannot be stopped.
as will the storm.
somewhere out there on the waters, over the storm-wracked shape of the Isle of Jura, a young rainbow is already waiting to play in the light, already saying *thank you,* with its presence.
i am wrapping this sign, this promise, around my shoulders.

my son, soft-soothing the things in his world

ever since his words found him waiting on the edge
of the world, my son, when asked to choose
between two things
—a favourite

go on, just choose one!

would close his eyes for a vernal moment
then shake his head, offering with his mouth
a choice shaped like kindness

i choose both of them!

never wanting to leave anything out
—leave anyone unchosen

opening his arms wide, he draws it all in
holds it close
loving all the things within his world

a gentle king

quietly unravelling the harm
that others have been given.

choose for yourself

the rain won't stay away forever. your angry drought will
break itself into a thousand sated memories.
in front of your weary eyes, the dog rose will bloom papery
again, weaving herself up the hedgerows to gain purchase.
a pale adoration of the light.
just before you want to give up, the heather will purple
herself all over your crags and fells.
a wide-eyed astonishment at your courage.

this is a common prophecy, waiting for its time.

when this happens, wrap your name three times around
your wrist, lest you forget that you are scarlet silk.
you are a soft thread of hope, worth everything, even loss.
perhaps, *especially loss.*
you will remember, and you will forget.
even in your thirst, you are an overflowing cup—a bare
wonder, wrapped inside a lucid life, always knowing
what it needs, always knowing what it holds.

this is a truth, waiting for you to believe it.

an elegy for the birds that roost on my limbs

if i don't turn my eyes away from the world outside my bones whilst the new light is still raw and fresh, all the honest birds that live within the wild forest on my limbs alight, and take off for distant countries, where they change, and try to fit in with the locals.
once they are there they do not want to stand out.
they do not want to draw attention to themselves.
they do not easily say words such as: *no, thank you. i have had enough of this. i choose my own life.*
they really want to say these words aloud, but they do not like to make a fuss, and so they quietly sacrifice their feathers just to keep the peace.
so, i choose my first moments carefully.
i deliberately pick up that wet word *choice*, and i plant it inside one of my first thoughts.
i let the light find me waiting, before i allow the world to kiss my cheek and oh, how it wants to! and on the days that i am stubborn and determined about this, all the roosting birds are allowed to wake up slowly, singing with their clear voices that sound like the waters of the Sound of Jura.
and they are all the shades of blue and all the shades of green. they are the colours of the sea foam and the racing, stormy waves. not having had to turn themselves invisible yet, their wingtips are shaped from new hope, which in turn blooms on the furry leaves of old hope.
i have to be reminded of this.
i so often forget what hope looks like just before it blooms. but also, they eat the memories of miracles for breakfast and when they move out of the trees and settle in my hair—some

preferring to nestle in the hollow at the base of my throat. i let them speak truth to me because they still know what God tastes like.
you might be surprised to know that this is an easy thing to forget, because there are so many bodies who want to give you their own God.
how they want to force the picture that they took of him into your unwilling hands.
they do not care that you do not recognise the face, or the eyes that don't resemble yours.
but i digress. i am so easily distracted.
most second-chance people are.
i want to eat beauty so that everything about my presence reminds others of hope. even strangers. even my own self.
i want to stop to talk to the moss and pay my respects to the buttery cowslips that go about their quiet business.
on mornings when i have missed them, the little birds in their morning coats—when in a moment of distraction, i allow them to slip through my fingers, they fly so fast, arriving to those new countries on their quick little wings.
once they are there, they forget where they grew up.
they forget the rich loam of my bones. their home.
little wars start to break out inside their feathery chests.
relentless little wars.
they try so hard to fit in.
they try their very best to give the locals, with their tattered snapshot pictures of their very own God, all the things that they demand.
and let me tell you this: some representatives of God, in their self-appointed positions, demand quite a lot.
eventually all the little birds grow entirely bald with grief.
a deep ache settles inside of them. it feels like something

they once knew but have since forgotten. a vague fluttering at the window. they forget how to sing and then they start to speak using only their second mouth.
the mouth that only knows how to be a smiling chameleon.
if you listen carefully, using your inner ears, you might hear the chameleons' lament on moonless nights.
what i am trying to tell you is important, so please listen.
when all of this has happened, it is difficult for me to call the birds back.
what i mean to say, is that i don't know *how* to call them back.
it is a small tragedy, really.
and then i have no choice but to wait for new birds to hatch from my grandmother's oldest prayers and i have to wait for the new birds to find their way back to my mouth.
this is loss. this is loss. this is loss.
if i don't turn my eyes away from the world outside my bones whilst the new light is still raw and fresh, all the honest birds that live within the wild forest on my limbs alight, and take off for distant countries, where they change, and try to fit in with the locals.
this is a long death.
inside their lukewarm little chests, they live smaller and smaller.
smaller even, than their smallest dreams.
this is a great sorrow.
eventually, their soft bodies forget everything that they once knew, except perhaps how to feed pieces of their own raw dreams to others.
and how to cut peace into small, sharp pieces.
and how to shape-shift into the body of a chameleon.
this is loss. this is loss. this is loss.
perhaps, you know this too?

dew

you will fall over your own feet one more time, rip the knee of your favourite jeans where they have grown thin, and on the way down towards the earth you will ask for a sign.
you will not be the first weary body to do this.
God is kept fervently busy with the business of signs.
some years ask for more than faith, and because we are flesh wrapped loosely around fragile bone, God knows that we need mothers to pick us up, despite the way in which we fold our flimsy wisdom into flags.
how we plant them smugly wherever we go, claiming God's mouth as our own.
God mothers us, and mothers us, and mothers us, despite what we have been told.
and isn't this what love does?
a heart folds itself away from things that refuse to introduce themselves by name.
you do not have to feel guilty about this.
how you hold yourself up by the skin of your hope.
how you tremble in front of the great unknown.
how you know that one more wrong move will tip you over the edge.
how you fear taking others with you.
the weight of knowing right from wrong.
the desperation for a sign.
but listen, there is nothing new under the sun.
you are not the first desperate body to hold out your hands.
the story goes that a man asked for dew in an unlikely place.
there is always a return to water.
how many times have you asked for moisture?
how many times have you wished away a clear night?

how many times have you held the wet fleece against your breasts, thinking that if you could only dry it with the heat from your own body, and look! it will be so.
it will be everything you have asked God for.
isn't this faith? did you know that a man once spoke to a valley of dry bones, and they came to life—filled up with breath right where they lay, and microscopic drops of water fell from their mouths. but first, before the miracle, he had to tell himself that it was alright to look like a fool.
i wonder if he feared his own failure.
the business of asking for signs is no place for an ego.
you have done this too, haven't you?
leaving pieces of yourself everywhere, hoping to be seen.
you stood there waiting, and waiting, and waiting, and you taught yourself new words that look like a taproot.
how you waited for it to breathe—the thing with many names. all of them sewn deeply into your being, weaved into the possibility of your fragile happiness, or into the flank of the grief that you did not want to know by its name.
how you heard it approaching in the distance.
how you turned your head away, so as not to look.
in the end you held it all bone-white in your closed hands.
decided to be brave.
decided to call it, *alive.*
if you held it at just the right angle, it almost appeared to be breathing.
almost.
isn't this faith? believing the dead to be alive?
a Lazarus, of some sorts.
i have done it too.
i know the notches on almost every bone in the body, the points of insertion, and the fossae that yearn to be full, or at the very least attached to something—perhaps the word, *love.*

maybe, that elusive paradise called, *chosen*.
but not all dead things want to come back to life.
some might just be sleeping. it happens.
but building a new house on the edge of a valley filled with *what-was-once-alive*, will cost you more hours than you have left and more life than you should ever give.
and if you were to look away for a small moment, you might see how your walls are filled with softness anyway.
you might notice how the afternoon light likes to sneak in through your kitchen window.
you might begin to see all the ways in which you are able to choose the shape of your own life.
you might find the place in which to plant the last seconds that you are given.
here is another small truth: you are running out of time, even now you are outgrowing your skin, and your life, and all the things that you have always thought were real.
all these things are slowly falling from you because you won't need them in the next room.
there, none of this will matter anymore.
you can't take much with you, except the names of the ones you love and the blue of a robin's egg.
even then, you might forget all of this.
but i don't know.
nobody really does, despite what is passed around the table as wisdom and certainty.
i have held the hands of people as they leave this place, but i haven't been there myself, so this is the wisest thing that i might say to you about death: that i simply don't know, but it finds its way into my words so often. death, is also life.
what else can i say that might be a balm to your heart?
not knowing what you want to know, is a heavy load to carry.
knowing what you *don't want to know*, is even heavier.

this is why God is kept busy with the business of signs.
some of us simply need to hold the answers in our hands.
this is all the faith that we can muster.
there is no shame in this.
this is for you, still searching wildly for an answer. when you wake up with water on your feet—the water that you asked for, run your fingers slowly over the sign that you have been given.
say, *thank you.*
lift your head and call yourself: *i-know-which-way-to-go.*
then, bring your hands up to the country of your mouth and taste your new truth.

is this the sign you have been waiting for

you ask for a sign?

tell me, is your heart soft in your hands?
is it satisfied?
does it ask for more?
does it still want more?
is it allowed to want more—to *hope* for more?

do you need to know anything else?

everything you see has been shown to you

in the buttery light of my kitchen, i draw a pot of tea, pour the milk into a jug, lay a tray, and then climb gratefully back into my warm bed.
just as i lift the cup to my mouth, God arrives with his dusty sandals, sits down on the bentwood chair that stands in front of my desk, smiles at me: *it's only me! the world is a bit upside down out there and i am here for your company.*
and me?
well, of course i start to cry because that is how i am wired.
my heart lives on the outside of my skin.
somehow, i have survived this gift.
i have also been given *you are too sensitive,* and *you are too focused on the details.*
for a long while, and for many hidden seasons, it hurt—this constantly being too much for others, although now that my life weighs much less, i have taught myself how to leave the words of others behind.
i drop them, like pebbles, by the side of the path.
there have been times when i have given my heart away too quickly, and not always to the right things, or even the right bodies. i wasn't always taught by others who knew what they were doing. i watched as they tried to fill their own wounds with what they scraped from the dirt in our front garden.
still, i have found my way around my own hungry heart and now i have a covenant with moss and the black ear of the pelt lichen living quietly off the death of things.
it is a love shaped to fit me.
but also, i have been fed grace, despite all the ways in which i have failed and there have been many.

but i have also been given love with no holy strings attached.
how a body made of love has shown me the weight of their promise, despite who i am, who i have been, and who i am still to become.
only love knows who i might be next year.
every day i am shown the meaning of the word, *unconditional.*
i am given all of this by another body shaped from dust, and love, and their own failures.
one who knows what it is to eat shame and fear, but who still chooses love.
the mercy in this sacrifice, holds me.
i have not often received this in a holy building, at least not without strings attached.
this is what i do know—that i have been given a life with someone who knows how to love, despite all the things that we were forced to carry with our bare hands.
and there have been many.
and somehow there was no safety net to catch us, and we knew loneliness, and we struggled, until we fell.
i try to tell him all of this—God who knows all about love and broken people, and who knows how to put them back together with a glue made of love and grace.
here, in my room, i try to use my words, but i cannot move.
all i know, is that holiness is sticking to me like honey and all i can do is breathe.
i do not stand up, and there is no music, no sermon, nobody stands as bridge, or go-between, or sin-eater, or sentinel.
it is just the two of us, *God-with-the-dusty-sandals*, and me.
and a holiness so wide and so full of light that i do not have a name for it.
and before i know it, the people arrive.
all the ones that i love and all the ones who love me.

they arrive behind my closed eyes, and my hands start to shape my words, and my words are water.
they are blessing, and blessing, and blessing.

and God speaks to my ordinary life, and i listen with all of my failures:

use your words! use them! use them! change names! change what you see right here on this weeping planet. change it into what you want to see.
use your words to undo and to unbreak.
you are part of me and i am part of you.
you are love. you are love. you are love.
bless the fine cracks in the foundations and the gaps in the crumbling walls.
where the pancreas has failed, you may soothe the dead cells.
speak tenderly to the ones that live. thank them for the work they do.
you are the keeper of holy words and the mouth that holds the key.
everything that you see has been shown to you. everything that you see has been thrown wide open for your trusting eyes to witness.
what will you do with this?

God leaves me sitting there—leaves to show someone else something that needs seeing, suggests one waiting body to another waiting body, somewhere out there.
all the soft bodies, with mustard seeds that need planting.
there are always things that need a blessing.
the soil is rich, the mouth is fertile, and the tongue is a small weapon that will bring life if it is allowed to.

God leaves me with all the things that need my love, leaves me with everything thrown into my lap. all the dry bones that i was beginning to give up on. he climbs out of my bedroom window to greet a grinning, coppery fox. with one last look over his shoulder, he reminds me to drink water, reminds me that i am salt, whispers:

go on!
it all lives inside your mouth.
what will you do with all that you are shown, today?

mantra for a guarded heart

softly, softly, watch how you step

soften the edges of your walls
moss them over, use your own hands for this

not everything that is sharp is your enemy

do you still remember where you keep the key
to your gates?

on learning to live again

and i saw how the holding on, the not letting go of things
—how this decision caused me pain
how not allowing my hands to fall wide open, naked
to the sky, how not trusting that i was held, nurtured
by something far bigger than *loss,* how this left me
unable to set free the thing
whose time had finally come to leave me

i was robbed of the quiet presence of common joy
i did this to myself

fear kept me blind to all the things that i stumbled past
—both beauty, and sadness
they both deserve to be felt with the whole body, both
deserve to be eaten with a hungry mouth

i missed so much beauty
because my eyes were afraid
to look away from the thing that was dying in my hands
lest i look down to find it no longer breathing

and then, allowing guilt to choose me as a home

i was so tired from breathing my life into something
that had long been ready to leave
that i had forgotten
how to live.

let me die a hundred rattling deaths today

just as i knew it would, it arrived with an old blade
well-whetted and thirsty
—the thing that i asked for, that i called by name

you might think that prayers are soft, flaccid things
feathery, and impotent

words waiting for higher approval

if you mean them, they are not

the silvery words that wait in the shallows
next to my tongue, are weapons

they know how to draw blood. they demand it often

here is my life wide open on the stone
how it has become the only offering that i own
the only thing that i can truly give to anyone

how it watches me from the other side of the room
how it watches to see what i might do
and i, woman-with-a-hungry-mouth
woman who is both child and crone
a weaver of circles, despite how i was taught to turn my
back on anything mysterious, anything
that cannot be defined

there are things i was not born into
where they now breathe whisper-soft in my hands
i made them by myself, from all that i was given
—the roots and the bitter herbs
that i did not sow with my own hands
the harvest that i refuse to reap every new morning
with my sleep-soft eyes

instead, i open my mouth wide and i bless my bleached
bones with black of raven and with blades of yew

let me die a hundred rattling deaths today, let me die
even, *seventy-times-seven,* times
to all the things that are not mine to carry

my life is watching
waiting to marry my words, waiting to dwell in sooth
yearning to stand on her own willing feet
holding only what is hers to carry.

this will be the beginning

every moment in which you spend your time as a shadow
of someone else, trying to fit in, trying to cut your days
from the same fabric as that of a stranger, is a lost moment.

listen!

your life knocks with a desperate insistence, begging for its
freedom.

you dwell within a famished world that is hungry for things
that are *real*, for things that do not hide.
it does not always realise what it craves—not the rush of
sugar, but the satisfaction of bread.

when you hide your face, and your past, and the honesty of
your days as they are right now, others miss out on your
beauty and the shape in which you have been stitched
together.

i am not sure you realise what a tragedy this is.
the slow, leaking loss of a person who is unlike anyone else.

give yourself the courage to be who you are.
you are a *now*, not a *tomorrow*.

be kind to others, but especially to yourself.
allow yourself the tender fear of being vulnerable, but also
remember to be a wise and boundaried place.

water your borders with quiet consistency. tend to the landscape of your solitude. if you don't know how to do this, find someone wise who might teach you. where there is work to do, do it.

if your exiled hands are forced to leave the familiar, you must find new mothers and new fathers, and in time you will become the unrelenting kindness that you once needed.

when they throw questions over your walls, like stropped hooks on a fishing line, know this—you do not have to explain how you arrived at your own front door.

the journey is yours alone. how you walked into your own life is not a public watering-hole.

you do not have to ask permission to leave a god that you were given.
you do not have to explain the name of the god that you hold in your mouth.

you do not have to explain. you only have to *love.*
your days are not a book for others to write their rules in.

open your arms wide to the world, but especially to soft things that breathe. close your ears to the noise.

teach yourself how to turn your gaze this way, and that. choose where you plant your time. choose it as carefully as how you choose the one to whom you give your heart.

time is not in great supply. a day has already been decided
where time will no longer yield to you.
the raven will call your name. you will not ignore it.
at long last, you will climb out of your earth-skin, and low
to the dew-wet grass, you will leave the husk behind.

you will move on to the other place.
the mystery of this is astounding.

we insist, with eyes that only see in part, on calling it by
different names. it doesn't matter. nobody really knows.
the more insistent ones attach God to it, peddling fear like
a currency.

there is no fear in love. God is love.

time is the gift. be careful how you use it. be careful to
whom you give it. you cannot get it back.

you might look at your days and see fissures and cracks.
you might feel tempted to fill them with stories that don't
ring true.
you might feel compelled to pour oil, or water, into the
glaring absence of what is left undone—an attempt to
smooth things over, to make things look like *more*
than the emptiness that you see from your side.

don't do it. don't let your own mouth do this to your life.
don't trade your past for false perfection.
don't let your eyes see your days as anything other than
what they are—a map of a life lived uncharted.

do not erase the imperfections.
let them be the beauty.
let them live as the true things that they are.

and what of these things that you have named, *failures*?
perhaps, even by your own hand you have painted the
small word, *sin*, on the pale length of your own flank?
or maybe even, *sinner*?

don't do this.
don't do this to yourself.
don't do this to the days that you have walked the dust of
this earth.

these are the things that set you apart, the things that allow
you to own your own name.
they will be many things, but they will be yours.

there is beauty in everything, but not everything is
beautiful. this is a lesson worth learning.

find the thread that holds it all together.
follow it with curiosity and eventually you will find yourself
right back where you started, only this time with kindness
in your eyes. a tenderness towards your own life.

your own hands holding the lantern for your own feet.
there is no fear in love. let this begin with you.

let things be what they are.
let them be honest.

let them be the marks on the once-bare map of your life.
perhaps, a warning to never return.

here be dragons!

but see how you swam with them.
how you crooned lullabies to them.
how you kept your head above the water.

never forget how you survived everything that tried to drown you.

how you did this without knowing how—without ever being *shown* how to do it.

how you respond to what you have been given, is already an offering. there is no fear in love.

you are loved.

see the white flags of a life attempting to make something of itself.

when it is dark, would you listen to it breathe?
would you allow it to be a peaceful presence curled up in the hollow of your neck?

say its name aloud until nobody can wrestle it from your fingers.

this, will be the beginning.

honeyed sweetness in a year called grief

when it finds you half dressed, finds you
without a plan for the rest of your life
grief wrapped around your neck
a feathered noose still pulsing

you might look up, turn your head to the sound
honeyed sweetness escaping the womb
the first song of last year's blackbird
thrown into the wind
winter, gently holding it to her breasts

you might not believe that even now
each note is being pinned to the velvet tips
of the goat willow tree bleeding yellow all over the path

you have come this far without a map
you can let go now, you might decide to slow down
open your eyes, perhaps believe that things might turn

listen!

the first song of last year's blackbird
is finding its way into your hands
wielding the blade
cutting the cord, the pulsing rope

this wild promise
this proof of life

what else do you need other than this?

this is a supplication dressed up as a poem

we are all secretly afraid of failing at something.
we have all made a meal out of fear.

every morning, you leave the shadowlands of your sleep.
your brain plump and watered.
your hands holding a couple of seeds.
perhaps, a thin prayer, or the tender shape of a mantra
that you speak with a hopeful mouth.
how you wave it in the face of everything lying in wait.
how you wield it against the great unknown.

you set off with hope for it all, only to return to yourself
hours later, the red dust of the backroads clinging to your
legs.

your pockets still full of everything unplanted.
the substance of things hoped for, now tangled up
in the wetness of your throat.

it is not the presence of *what-you-might-fail-at*, roaming within
your borders, but what you allow it to do whilst it dwells
there, that robs you. again, it is not the *presence* that captures
your courage, but how much ground it is allowed to cover.

perhaps, you have fallen for a lie?

what of the times where you were so afraid to fail that you
chose not to begin. the only way out of the *fear-that-entangles*
is to make the first mark. just do it. there is no other way.

if this is the day that your breath is at last unmade, what would you regret? of course, there would be words left unsaid and love unrequited. but listen, every graveyard is full of the ancestors' bones and their long-dead potential. untold dreams lie buried in that soil.

again: what would you regret?

there it is. it has just climbed inside your head, and you want to let it out of your mouth. it has a name. say it.

it doesn't matter where you have come from.
we are all held together by our scars.
we are all a thousand stories.

it matters that you make your life count for beauty.
it matters that you leave portions of kindness in unlikely places.

something that a stranger might feast on.
something that they might even break their fast on.

scratch it out in the dirt if you must.
even God used spit, and dust, and mud.

are you afraid of failure, or the acid opinions of strangers?

you, with your singular ephemeral life—why would you care what others think of how you serve yourself plates of joy?

do not give your life to anybody else.

do not give another body a space in which to live inside your head, even if they are bodies who love you.
they have their own inner lives to tend.
they have their own spacious place to find.
this is a good rule.

here is the thing: if you dream of writing a story then do it.

if you dream of painting, or of singing, or a hundred other things that you hold inside your bones, it is as simple as this—just do it.

begin. begin. just begin.

the world has never needed beauty as much as it does right now.

there is a groaning, and a weeping, and a deep hunger.

listen to me! already you are an entire book.
already you are all the stories of your ancestors.

if you were to stand very still, your spine stretched long and certain along the listening body of a horse chestnut tree, all the stories will find you. they will speak to you from within the leaves, from deep within the rough mesas of bark.

it matters that you start.
it matters that you water *the-thing-that-you-were-given*.
it matters that you don't water *the-fear-that-you-will-fail*.
it matters that you make things at your kitchen table, even whilst the dinner is cooking, or the dishes are soaking.

do you feel that you need a special place where you can
work undisturbed outside of your home? you don't.
a studio is a rare thing. they are not that important.
i only have a door to a room that i dare not close.
i chase my words with one ear to the ground, listening for
the sound of a small body needing me.

this too is a creative life. this too, *breathes.*
perhaps it is judged as inferior, by some who don't live
within the borders of my life. it doesn't matter to me.
their opinions are not important.

it matters that i choose to create a thing that no other body
could ever replicate.
it matters that someone, somewhere, is waiting to see what
falls from my hands—perhaps a child.
they do this—small humans, always watching to see what
they should be afraid of and what they should welcome.
always building their future with their eyes.

but what if it is a man of ninety-nine, who has been waiting
for permission to write it all down. how he lived his life on
his own ordinary terms. how he met his great love, or
perhaps, how he lost them. what if he has waited to draw
the secret world behind his eyes, never having given his
name to *courage.*

shall we imagine a world without his story being told?

all sorts of things might have happened to him. perhaps his
voice was strangled by a war, or a death, or the sheer force
of simply trying to stay alive.

that relentless chipping away at brick walls.

listen.

it matters that you face the unknown.
it matters that you face the wilderness within you.
it matters that you try.

oh! what have i done here? would you look at this!

this is not a poem. it never was.

it is a supplication. a petition. a plea.

perhaps, a call to war.

tell me, what will you do with it?

we are always children caught in adult bodies

i want to make beauty with my life. i want to shape beauty *from* my life and leave it behind for others, perhaps to soften the blow of my short existence, or maybe, i want to erase my sharp edges. perhaps, to dull the blade that others have cut themselves on, whilst loving me.
there are things that i have done, the weight of which is quite astounding. quite suffocating. there were times where i have made decisions based on what i thought was the right thing at that moment, often with no guide, and no oracle at my side. it does not mean that i would do the same things again. there are many things i would run from now.
i can think of many, but there are also others that i can call to my side by their rare names. you will not recognise them because you have not had to hold them up to your mouth to taste them with your unwilling mouth.
i did these things in the midst of a hurricane, caught in an avalanche of emotions and circumstance, with nobody there to show me how to eat the risk—how to butter the fall-out and consume it as bread. as sustenance.
some of it still matters. there are ripples, and ripples, and ripples that circle out from my greatest failures.
most of it has mercifully faded away.
i have been given grace in portions too great for me to ever finish. it is piled onto my plate and overflows onto the table. even when i have turned my face, when i have tried to refuse the kindness and the love, especially then.
what i mean to say is this: we are always children caught in adult bodies. we are constantly struggling towards something that will fill the hunger and ease the ache.

we hurt others, and we hurt ourselves, but there is still beauty everywhere, waiting with open hands to soften the sharpness we surround ourselves with. ready to knit a soft covering for the edge of the razor blade that we call our past.
when we make things from nothing, we are writing a story. we are giving our own lives a life.
we are holding what was once hidden, up to the light, just as it falls through the kitchen window.
on some endless afternoon, a stranger might stumble across it unexpectedly. perhaps when we drop a stray word at their feet. all the parts of us that we think we are sowing on failed ground, but oh! how the mysterious breathes all around us.
in that feathered moment, their words might not know how to get dressed, or what to wear for the occasion.
all their sentences will stay naked and silent; words caught in the back of their throat.
they will look at it with their five-year old eyes.
they will exhale.
recognition will break quicksilver through the cage of their chest, breaking the bars of the prison.
stooping low to gather the holy dust from the ground, they will carry it with them for the rest of their days, pulling the memory of it from their pocket, every now and then.
they will chew on the edges of that moment in which they were seen—that day, on which they felt less alone.
i want to make beauty with my life.
i want to shape beauty from my life and leave it behind for others to feast on.
i want to leave tender letters in the wild for other struggling bodies to find, not so much to be understood, but to allow others to understand their own shape. their own light.
this is my two small coins. my offering.

look at you, finding beauty everywhere

how she dwells low to the ground
how she lives close to the light
waiting to be broken open
waiting for anyone with eyes to see
waiting for the hungry to come searching

and you, undoing a thousand things
with your ravenous, cupped hands.

God, inside the walls

i am not particularly good at reading maps, or at following directions once they have been handed to me reverently by another breathing body.
and i turn down the insistent voice on the satnav when i am driving, because my hearing is the keenest and most curious sense that i possess, and i can only find my way by drowning out the noise that is thrown at me.
and before i was given this body and this life, already there was God, present and breathing within the permeable walls of the mystery, holding the egg that i once was and crooning a grandmother-song softly over the curve of each small malleus. breathing wild God-breath onto each stapes and folding the incus *just so* with knowing hands that smell like red raspberry leaf, meadowsweet, and yarrow for the healing after. God, who already knew the dark shape of each fierce *valley-of-the-shadow-of-death* waiting for me, and who with the heart of a mother-god, blessed me with the vigilant ears of a small owl.
and they don't tell you this in church, because it takes too long to read all the rules and the regulations, and they have to spend a lot of time making sure that nobody gets lost any further—that nobody wanders off to places where they cannot be seen or heard by the *people-who-are-important.*
but it was always within my bones to go searching, to get lost, and to fall down a hundred times a day, down to where i could listen to the moss breathing on the old dry-stone walls, my head somehow always inclined to hear the stories that lichens tell a body who is not afraid of losing her way.
because getting lost is what i am good at and being found is

what God has always been good at, although never in the places where they tell me to look, them preferring to give me a God that follows their rules, and who speaks with their voice, and who agrees with all their sermons with a godly nod, and me—always being rebellious, albeit quietly so.
my small, owl-ears always pricked to the presence of danger.
i am a wombed mammal, who listens for things that breathe.
i am only a soft-breasted body, making a life for herself by searching dry fields for wet membranes, and for the damp promise of dew, on a fleece called, *i-am-desperate.*
now, i only search for things that are seldom found inside buildings, especially the ones that are called, *holy*. all those walled structures, holding *bodies-also-made-of-dust.*
bodies, who only know one version of God, and how to feed him to those who don't know that they aren't hungry, until it is almost too late. i am a rebellious body, who is not afraid of losing her way. getting lost is what i am good at, and being found is what God is good at, although never in the places where they tell me to look.

the time for telling the beginning is near

some of us are quietly mending our well-worn lives, with the old threads handed down by women, who walked the skin of mother earth before us.
silk, and cotton, and blood-stained rope.
how they still make radiant marks on all that remains of the day. all that remains of us.
some of us pray by making tea in the dark hours before the light climbs lithe and long-legged down the drainpipe and in through the kitchen window.
a prayer and a spell are the same thing really, each one just wearing a different coat.
if you mean what you say when you say them, they are both weapons, so use them well. be wise. be humble. be brave.
think carefully about the life that you want your words to create once they have left the boundaries of their home.
we carry medicine in our wet mouths by crooning the names of all the willing healers—rosemary and sage, and mugwort and dandelion.
how they wait to be called closer.
how they wait for a finger crooked in anticipation.
we know the name of the sycamore as a holy thing and the yew as a temple without walls.
we do not need bricks and doors.
some of us fight our quiet wars by lighting small flames in windowsills every afternoon, their warmth felt only by the soft bodies that dwell within the country of our home—the kingdom in which we have given God a bed to sleep in, a chair in which he sits reading poems to the holy crones with moss in their bleached hair.
how they weep at the sound that rises from the lungs of the

earth—the low lament and the groaning. how they wonder amongst themselves, over bread and sour wine, whom they might send out into the wild to pull the scraps of wool from the thickets, and the lost threads of courage from the spindly thorn of the bramble.
some of us make it a habit to be the light—how we wrap ourselves in peace at the end of each moment, learning to inhale the cup of air that lives inside the pause. that thin place where things are often lost. see how our fingers are bleeding from refusing to let go of beauty. how we turn our face the other way. we choose to do this. some of us will not be distracted from love. we will not allow our mouth to become a womb for war. other mothers' children are worth more than a stone-in-the-hand.
and i am the mother of a boy-child, who is becoming a man. do not think for a moment that i am not paying attention.
i am my grandmother's grandmother and my name does not belong to anybody else.
it is peace, and peace, and peace, and i am a map to the valley where the oak moss softens the rough edge of winter.
i am a way marker on the path to the watery wet where the flag iris sets herself on fire, and where the field mouse wraps herself around the furry shapes of her babies.
i will not allow myself to be marked and numbed by all the distractions that shimmer, and glitter, and catcall.
the screeching voices of small screens, magazines, and all the bloated newspapers.
i will not allow my ears to belong to the impotent voices of power-guzzling men who plant lies in the hedgerows.
no.
i choose life.
some of us pull pulsing choices from our frayed pockets, up to *seventy-times-seven,* times a day.

we are scarred healers. we remember what we were told.
how to break free. how to keep our freedom.
we turn away from the noise, so that we might see what they do not want us to see.
we look for the fear on the other side of someone's fight.
we look for the flight behind someone's fear.
and you, how you keep on folding your numbed heart into a too-bright paper crane.
how you tell yourself, *just-one-more-time.*
how your fingers know the sharpness of each edge.
how you spend your days hoping for that one thing that you need, that one person, or the numbers that will make it all better—the shape of that unborn miracle you are too afraid to hope for and yet you fall asleep saying its name.
you eat small portions of faith in the dark hours and then deny it all three times in the light.
some of us listen for the clear bell of a blue tit's song ringing in another country.
hearing all the words that are not said.
some of us listen with our hands on the belly of the earth.
we are midwives-in-waiting.
we wait for what we know will come, because the weight is too much too bear and the stories are crying out to be told.
all the ancestors are holding up their babies and on nights when the air is liminal, the gone grandmothers are dancing around the fire, their skirts hitched high, their patience as thin as a bride's veil, their voices rearranging the atmosphere.
freedom will marry longing and bloom bright on our tongues and we will have new words for all the old stories.
time is a pregnant moon, and her waters are about to break.
and we are waiting for our ancestors to be born right into the fabric of our stories.
the Spirit is alive.

some of us are stitching all the secrets into place.
some of us are making space for truth and we are not afraid of tender weapons.
we have seen this all before.
we are young, but we carry old. we breathe ancient air.
we are the stories from long before there were gardens.
we are wild stories and ancient paths.
we are the cool sea mist, laced with ocean salt.
we are the story tellers—the ones who birth, and the ones who listen for the sound of death when she sends the sleek raven with the final message.
listen!
it is the time for things to begin and it is the time for things to end.
now is the time to pull the small coin of faith from the velvet lining of your inner ear.
be eyes and ears wide open, to the sage-smoky voices of the grandmothers of the great-grandmothers, as they wait for the stories born a long time ago to get up off their mat and start walking on their healed legs.
be eyes and ears open, to what breathes unseen, as we wait impatiently for the words to arrive fierce and soft-feathery.
prophecies ready to be stitched onto the waiting skin of the sighing earth.
all the old prayers and all the old spells, waiting to stand up and be claimed by name.

for such a time as this, we are here.

listen. listen. listen.

unfettered

when i open my window to the first inhale
the gulping rush of it, the vaporous tide
the night still clinging to the back of my neck
—it is God, on his happy feet, dancing before me
having finally escaped all the holy pages
throwing open the curtains wildly to everything

laughing aloud in his tattered loin cloth:

see! i told you so! we are still alive! we live!

how wondrous!

all the sleeping answers

on my way to the shop to buy apples and milk, i find God
just around the corner, eyes closed to the world, head held
low to the ground, his hair wild, he is long-legged
in faded denims, and smiling dimple cheeked
the air that surrounds him was once a mountain stream
when he speaks, his breath smells like the heather
that blushes the cheeks of the Campsie Fells
he tells me that he is listening to the daffodils resting
amongst the roots of the sycamore tree
how they have just now woken up
he tells me that they are busy choosing their favourite
colours—the exact shade of yellow each one wants to be
how the weight of this work makes him pause in wonder
he tells me that this is his favourite time of year, the earth
breaking open like an old prayer, showing the world
her secrets, how he likes to see hidden things
find their way to the light
he tells me if only i knew of all the wondrous things that
happen away from my eyes
all the quiet astonishment
all the sleeping answers
that arrive in their own time, *on time*
i would wrap trust more tenderly around my wrist
i would secure the knot a little tighter
on that scarlet thread holding the story together
with his water-wet voice he tells me, that if only i walked
through my life, with my sensible eyes dressed up
in their wild boots, and their fairy tale coats
i would never eat fear again.

what if you were to treat this as your last day

what if you were to let go of all the frayed notions
of what happiness should look like.

see—here is a wide-open day
already broken into pieces, small enough
to fit inside your waiting hands.
here is your breath
still thrumming faithfully
against the pink walls of your chest.
you might want more than you have already been given.
perhaps, grass under your bare feet and a clay pot of earth
to call your own.
maybe, you only hunger for a life
beneath a wild expanse of stars. a life
that you have seen sitting snug on the shoulders of others.

listen—the soft sound of your days are tiptoeing towards
the door, saying:

now! now! now!

this is all that you have.

anything else is still waiting to be given, is still not ready
to find its way to you—might never be yours, although
with your sure voice, your firm voice, you call it:

tomorrow.

this is how i make a life

it is like whistling in the valley-of-the-shadow-of-death
—telling my eyes where to look, and my ears
what not to listen to.

see how i stitch a weapon from the word, *choice.*
see how i wage soft little wars, a hundred times a day.

how my mouth, is a tender war machine.

a soft March morning

here is the first playful breeze
climbing in through the window
teasing the bed sheets, sleep-shaped and memoried
the thin skin of my eyes, the contour of each clavicle
each fine hair suddenly alive, a current of promise
here is my tea in a porcelain cup
—my favourite
the gold rim, the way that my hand curves to receive it
like cradling the unexpected, a wanted thing, new and alive
and if you knew to listen for it, from deeper inside my
house, these safe womb-walls, there radiates
the soft sighs of my son, swimming to the edge of his
dreams, sleep quietly releasing him
to slay dragons once again.

messengers

on the seams of Stobhill hospital there is a place
where thinly veiled veneer yields to the wild, and there
i saw a fox
her amber eyes holding mine for a hundred searching years.

it escapes me now—the detail of time.
i was barely breathing, for fear of stripping the spell.

when she had given me enough, she tip-tip-tipped her tail
and slow-danced her slinky body into the undergrowth.

to share space with the warm body of a wild mammal
—something to soften the edges of a day.
and two days. even three.
something sinuous and enthralling.

a startling gentleness.

later, back inside my tame life, i dance hesitantly with sleep.
i am hungry for rebirth. for things i didn't know i wanted.

the vixen's coppery gift.

in the distance, where untamed things still dwell, i am
given the back-and-forth of two owls, their bodies
stitched into the night sky, reminding each other
where to look—where to swoop low for what they are
about to receive.

surrogate

far away from the bones of all my dead
i am a life buttressed by lean roots
i walk the long grass of a graveyard
with only my empty mouth as a friend

on quiet days there are rabbits criss-crossing their way
through the stones
and deer, always startled by the weight
of keeping their lives safe, the unexpectedness of it
the things that nobody told them
and a robin, marking the map of the old headstones
with his feathered diligence
they know me by now, my presence
how we are all fed here, always low to the ground
searching for things that fill
they watch how i gather myself, my mammal body
my foreign throat, always picking out names that know me
stroking the vowels and the flanks of each consonant

when i find an *Anna-beloved-grandmother*
and a *Daniel-brother-and-son-taken-too-soon*

i stop, and hold them close to my chest
i say to all the bodies lying still within the earth:

you are not mine, and i am far from the bones of the ones i love

will you let me hold your name in my hungry, mourning mouth?

choice

show me the things that have kept you hidden
all your shadows, and the stories that you have stitched
into a life, and the life that you are stitching
into a story

even now, you are deciding what to keep
all the words that you have pinned to your spine
the downy feathers that you pluck from your own breast
to soften what you were given

how carefully you choose them, how brave you are
to keep searching for a way out

you are making a place in which to live

be ruthless, be brutal
for this you need to wield an honest knife

if you only keep one word
let it be true
start with your own name, all the things
that you call yourself

it doesn't have to be the letters you were given
once upon a time
when you were still fresh from the dark waters
the home you left, the serous softness
the womb of your mother, her hunger
and later, all the unlived lives of your father

did you know there once was a man called, *sorrow*
destined for grief, but he said:

no

simply refused what he was given, stood tall
before all that was holy, said:

i will not live broken, i know there is more to this

held up his hands, waiting
like a child
and it was done
given to him
this grace

so why not you?

empty your pockets, rip the seams
start over, start a new name, carve it out
carve it deep
whatever you do
own it
hold onto it with both hands
hold it up
let everyone see how you choose
your own skin, your days
how you fold your life into something
new
over and over
the beauty of this
the wonder

may i bless you with something?

you have been given a tender defence
a stronghold
a weapon

choice.

when you were David

will it really matter
in a hundred flowering years from now—the thing
that makes its home deep inside your head, its dark nest
balancing just so—watch out! it might fall, and then?
who might you be without its presence, without
the script it keeps scribbling for your life.

will it really count for something worth dragging with you?

this is a small truth:

tomorrow might not even draw a full breath, might not
breathe at all, does not even exist yet.

it is not yours.

soon you will be the next one
to walk through that curious door, escaping the cocoon
that you call:

my life.

and then? think carefully. will it really matter?

instead, how about this:

this evening, how you silenced yourself, turned your face
towards it all, how you stood untroubled
in front of the bedroom window, watching the sky

set herself on fire.
her steady blueness. her azure face, gloriously unveiled.
all fancied up in her going-out dress, the sun
wearing her salmon-pink stilettoes, her purple hair.

and all this just to say:

i am off! goodnight! don't wait up!

shameless around the edges—her slow, brazen exit.
without a care for anyone watching, catching her leaving.

and you witnessing.

how you were David, unable to tear your eyes away.
unwilling.

that if this were sin, you were all in.

that you wanted it, ate it up, licked your fingers, wanted
more.

that you said:

for what i have just received, thank you. thank you. thank you.
i want more!

all your lives are waiting to breathe

have you asked it yet?
that well of restlessness that stirs inside of you.
have you asked it what it wants from you?
have you asked its name?
it knows yours.
knew it, even before your bones started to knit themselves together.
it is as old as you are, and it is older.
it knows your father.
it knows the sound of your grandmother's heartbeat in the womb of her own mother.
it is *this* moment, but not the one still to come.
you have not been given that yet, and you might not get to hold it in your hands, so listen carefully.
love deeply. don't waste time.
this gift is older than the moon, and it knows you.
it knows the shape of everything that you want to give.
listen.
it breathes.
have you asked it yet?
that well of restlessness that aches inside of you.
have you asked it what it wants you to do?
lie down on the grass. the earth. the kitchen floor.
it doesn't matter where, just lie down, so that for one
gossamer moment, you are unable to see your life
as you insist on seeing it.
lie down, so that your body is held by a force far
greater than all your fears.

lie down, so that you might begin to see
how all your fears could never weigh more
than the breath of the things you hope for.
look at the words living behind your eyes.
look at the pictures of your life.
all your past lives in their little windows.
look at all that you have been given.
hold it up to the light.
count the things that have left you.
remember the things that you had to give up, but especially
the things that you did not *want* to give up
—the things that were taken from you.
count their loss.
ask for their names.
hold them in your mouth.
then, get up from where you were buried, and tell of it.

things you will miss if you carry on hiding

how you walked the earth holding your softness
the wide-open spaces you have had inside of you
since you were still new in your unlived skin.
how you trusted the hand that reached for you.
how you didn't sniff at it first, to see if it spoke the same
words as the eyes that it belonged to.
it wasn't your fault. you didn't know, but you learnt.
drew back. hid yourself.
you could have picked up a stone, taken aim. you didn't.
there is kindness in that decision.
it takes courage to choose kindness over war.
you are not stupid for believing their lies.
you are not stupid for trusting that someone wouldn't hurt
you. you have a hundred names for yourself and none of
them are kind. you could carry on hiding, but you might
miss the quiet footsteps of another soul who, perhaps
only today, decided to shed their fear too.
you might miss their voice calling from within a thicket
of trees.
you might never know what it feels like
to hear another body, say your name
the way it was always meant to sound
—like wonder, falling from the lips.
you might be the one they have been waiting for their
entire life. the one that they hoped was out there.
the one that fits.
look! the robin is sitting on the old stone wall, waiting for
you to notice the red flash of his chest, waiting for you to
eat the miracles caught up in the morning fog.
let the light fall on your scars. come out now.

you are everything that they never wanted you to be.
you are everything that they always wished they could be.

wait for it. listen.

listen to the sound that your name makes when it climbs up someone's throat, wrapped in awe.
the heather is blooming in your hands and your name is etched all over your life.

courage.

beauty is a weapon too

the sweet peas
that trail along the fence at the bottom of the garden
didn't plant themselves, you know.
they had to come from somewhere.
i had to decide what to do with my eyes, had to choose
where to put my hands.
i chose to bury them in the dirt.
i could have gone searching for blood and bone
i could have used each breath that i have been given
as a weapon.
i chose instead, to carry water.
life is always wet when it breathes.

and i chose this—to sit outside the back door, to be
the first to see the light as it falls on a new-born leaf.
remembering it all so that i can tell of it again.

someone must be the softness
for a world returning from war.

all gussied up

the evening sky gussying herself.
stars glittering her party face.
a crescent moon slung low over her shoulder.

giving my son an unbound life

i point my index finger towards the light.
with my hands, i show him where to start the search.
the bulk of an aeroplane slices the greatness of the sky.
the map on his bedroom wall shouts questions at us, hints
at mystery.
all day long the words, *where to next,* are thrown around.
like glitter it sticks to everything we do.
at the far-off sound of the night train shoof-shoofing
along, i wonder aloud at its destination—push the question
across the table. i serve it with chocolate milk and toast.
together we think up stories for the ones inside its belly.
at breakfast i ask:

i wonder what porridge tastes like in India.

curiosity dangles from my hands, i peddle mouthfuls of
adventure, a constant travel guide—even when it seems
unlikely, especially then, i empty a bag of bones
in front of his hesitant feet.
how they chinkle-chankle with promise.
how they smell like miracles.

let us see what generosity the world holds for you.

moment by small moment, i am always doing this work.
my dog-eared prayers, folded into faith.

i say: *you are a new life.*
i say: *you are your very own.*
i say: *i do not want you searching for the things that i have lost.*

November

hugging the thin bones of a wintering hedgerow
with my body
being careful with each thing that will soon be a memory
—the small anchors of your tomorrow
the part of your life when i will be gone from your view

walking this wildness
i am at once a great tenderness to myself
a kindness, that i carve deliberately
from the honesty of my life
i push away the guilt that snaps at my heels

the weight of each lacy second that still hangs
attached to my name, the size of each choice still left to me

how they thin, grow translucent, more valuable
than any gold i might be given
by any hand

what i have, each new day, is this raw gift
pulsing in my hands
—time, and i will give all i have

in the topmost branch of a tree there was a raven
jet black and ancient, and rain so fine i could barely feel it
but for the wind

and off to the right, in a farmer's dormant field
half a diluted rainbow planted itself unsecured, still
it was a sign

and so, i grabbed it for both of us with my greedy hands

without you even noticing it, i shall pull it over us
in the days to come

from now on i shall choose what i choose more carefully
my days a nest of moss and feathers, my days
a home

being careful with each thing that will soon be a memory

even in your oldest days, how i want them to be full and
rich
always on your bedside table, within easy reach of your
fingers
how i want them to smell like ripe pears, like love
still warm in the hollow of your neck

even when you are old and grey, and i am gone from your
sight, especially then.

this will be enough

what is it to be honest with a life?

to allow the body of it to be picked clean
to not hide from the death of things
to dwell within its emptiness
to feast within its fullness
to plant a sycamore
a wild, white rose
fragrant
despite the taste of your famine
to watch it rambling over each bare bone
allowing the wonder of it all to live inside your mouth.

how not to drown

my life wants to tell you something which i think
you already know, but we forget things
when we are trying not to drown, we only know
how to eat the air.
how to look like we are swimming, like we are having
a good time out there, flailing in the rough waters.

i want you to know that i see you.
let me slip you a rope made from all the words that i give
to myself when i am about to fall.
they are well-worn, but strong.

i have made a life out of this—out of slipping
and falling over my own feet.
they say that it's only failure if you stay down.
if you don't get up.

let me tell you this:

there have been times that i stayed down for so long, that
the earth moulded her loamy self to my shape.
i did not resist her.
eventually, a moss woman found me.
in that darkness she velveted her verdant self
around the guilt that i had wrapped around my wrist.
the sycamore's leaves covered my limbs.
the rain fell, watered the seeds
that i could not see with my eyes.

seeds like tiny mouths, shaped like my grandmother's
great-grandmother's brazen prayers. old and grey, they are
words that go out daily with strong baskets.
words that know that they have work to do.
words that wait for just the right moment.
time needs to be ripe and ready.

it was never about anyone else.
i have not always known this. this is not selfish.
it is honest. it is how love works. at least, it is how love
begins. to love your own being first, is rich soil
for more love to grow on.

i had been fed so many lies about what it really meant to
love. i have not always known that it starts deep inside my
own velveting bones.

when i had travelled inside myself long enough, the moss
woman called me back. a blackbird broke through the quiet
and threw a song wildly into the night.

this is the grace that i have eaten, my mouth stuffed
with every sharp thing that i have named, *wrong.*
there have been many and most of them were growing on
my own limbs.

i did not know how to hold myself up to the light.

even then, love has never left me.
this is how love works.
this is what love does when its body is a real thing.

eventually all the numbness that was living inside my bones
started swishing, and hissing, and fizzing.

my voice found me again. i was glad of this. when you hear
me now, you will hear leaves, and lichen, and trees.

and this is the truth that the moss woman told me:

sometimes, what i have called, *dead*, God has called, *sleeping*.

even me. i have been dead many times.
i am so many rebirths, so many new things. so lush.
so much green. not every soft body will admit to this.
i have stopped judging the borders of my own life
by things that do not fit me. not every soft body will
respect this. there are bodies who would watch you drown.
they have not found their way into the earth, have not
heard the moss woman, have not felt her touch.

still, my life would like to tell you something:

you do not have to pretend that you are swimming.
you do not have to pretend at all.
you cannot fail at this because life is not a test.
sometimes, the water is deep, but the earth is a soft place.
a womb. the original home. if you are there. stay there.
do not struggle. do not resist. just keep breathing.
keep listening for the way to the hidden roads.
your life is greening itself deep in its wintering.
it is only sleeping. it is not dead. wait for it.
it lives.

what you were beginning to forget

it is easy to forget the sound of small birds singing. we forget to listen. the dawn chorus arriving. the bravest ones soothing the dark skies with their seed-songs. all the noise competing with their fresh morning prophecies. calling us to remember. calling us to not forget. in all the places that we walked, there were robins on mossy walls—plump flashes of red from within the tangled ribs of hedgerows. all the feathered messengers with bells in their pulsing throats and we were there to see them. to witness. we knew this as a gift. we knew it for what it was. and the morning after the storm—the coal tit losing its way, suddenly separated from the familiar wildness. choosing the wrong way. how you closed the bedroom door behind you—the room at once smaller. the escape route more certain. how the same hands that soothed the scraggy barn cat the day before, captured the small body in flight, cradling every part of the feathered fear. the joy etched on your face as you watched it fly away. your body listening for the signs you were beginning to forget. all the promises you were ready to give up on. how it settled nearby. proclaimed its freedom. how you knew it for what it was. your life gratefully receiving the new promise. reminding yourself to not forget.

love does what love does

i have always been good at getting lost.

the God that i was given never liked this—my knack for running away, this rebellion of falling in love with things that are hidden.

i was made this way—shaped in my mother's womb from a hundred fierce questions.

a bent for finding myself in places that others do not want to be in, purposefully folded into my bones.

a holy act, or perhaps, a map.

after i run away for the last time, i find a different God searching for me in the bramble bushes.

there is nobody with him.

he has come for me on his own.

i do not recognise his face, or at first, the language that he speaks. but i know that he is kindness, that in his mouth there lives a hundred truths, and each one gentle.

smoothing my wildness with his proud hands, he helps me up, tells me his real name, tells me:

go—get lost again. don't look back. i am love. i will find you.

waterlily warfare

everything is ok. everything is ok.
and i am shaping a prayer out of the thinnest air.
out of the atoms that bind me to the place where my bones
grew to fit my skin, and my skin stretched to fit my bones.
and isn't it all a wild miracle how we are still here.
how we are still breathing.
and there have been more than a few *once-upon-a-time* times
that had sharp edges, and so i know that i can do this. i know
what i can live through.
i have been given several other lives that saw me stunned at
what-i-did-not-see-coming. it is so easy to slip fear over my
shoulders. it fits me so well.
if you were here next to me as i write this, i would lean
in close and whisper into the pinkness of your ear.
i would tell you the names of the things that find me when i
am drinking tea, or making lunch, or taking a boy-child to
the dentist.
i would not say their names aloud.
they might think that i am calling them.
i only want to tell you how they follow me on their clay feet.
how they move so fast holding their heavy chains.
how they chinkle-chankle when i turn to look at them.
fearsome.
and i would tell you about today, how when i stopped by the
loch, her green waters soupy, and how there were swans.
how they kept one of their babies alive. only one.
there is always the sleek presence of foxes about, don't you
know—other watchful mammal mothers with babies whose
empty bellies also need filling.

we do not like to think of this, do we?
but here is a sharp truth: not everything works out the way that we want it to.
we are always sharing our breathing space with loss.
still, somehow one swan baby survived.
and isn't it all a wild miracle how things just keep on living.
how we are still fighting, and some days, quietly flourishing.
and those things that know how to find me, even them, even they know how to keep breathing.
i make it so easy for them.
they use my own mouth.
they eat my own words.
this is how they live.
i want to tell you how they sat themselves down on the splintered body of a fallen oak tree. all those things that remind me of *what-i-should-fear.*
all those things that remind me of *what-might-still-happen.*
they have always been so patient, swinging their hairy legs in the thin wintery light.
how they waited to see what i would do next.
how they waited to see if my hands would remember how to waterlily themselves into a soft weapon.
a blade called, *please* and *thank you.*
small words that are a strong defence against their wiles.
a palisade. a strong place.
i want to tell you how, when they laughed at me, i told my eyes to look away.
to look at the light and at nothing else.
i want to tell you how my mouth is a doubting, common prophet knocking on God's back door to ask for water.
even as i wait for the wine to find my cup.
even as i swallow everything that i am afraid of.

the brazen amen

it is possible to imagine it all working out.

how i plant the seeds deep inside my head, far behind
my doubting eyes. how i water them with the words
inside my mouth.

the fierce tending.
the relentless, *thank-you.*

how i stubbornly prepare the table, for what has not
arrived yet.

stewing apples on a Monday afternoon

after i bring them home
i ignore the world for at least an hour.
as if i were the very tree that grew them
i croon: *aren't you a beauty.* my hands are full of green.

a friend, who has music living inside her mouth, and who
knows the ways of food and happiness, tells me:

keep the skin if you are able. it adds more goodness.

and to this, i add cinnamon and plump little raisins
and a generous teaspoon of marsala.
in front of the range i am deep inside my life.

stirring the waters, i am tending to the light.
some things will not be rushed.

for three days i will feast on the sweet.

a home within your failure

you are tall windows that let in all the light.
when nobody is watching, you are music.
you dance along the fault lines of your life.
this, is courage.
look at you—how it spills from your front door!
down the path it goes, and out into the world.
every small moment you can find, you hold the holy in
your hands.
and then, you set it free.
it knows your name.
somehow, it always finds its way back to you.
and when it does, i hope it settles in the curve of your neck
—a handful of wonder.
i hope that you let it. i hope that you turn your cheek
to feel its softness, feel it choosing you.
you only have one long breath in which to live.
a brief exhale.

call yourself, *brave.*
call yourself, *beautiful.*
call yourself, *wanted.*

use your own voice for this. it might take a little while
to recognise but do it. be faithful about this.
you are a wild thing. a free thing. a soft thing.
an intriguing thing of many parts. a curious complexity.
if you have not been fed, it might feel easier to look away.
—to exist hungry. it is not.

there are things that one can do nothing about.

life will climb roughshod into the cage of your chest.
but also, there is beauty. look for it.

eyes open. eyes open. eyes wide open.

i hope that tall trees grow all over your life.
and lilacs, brassy and bold.
may their sweetness purple your walls.
may bees come, and caterpillars, and other small beasts
holding prophecy in their names.
may they make their home within every failure
you will ever own. may they never leave.
and in the evenings, when you are alone
with your darkness, may you be kind to your whole life.
you will need to learn how to do this.
—each sharp corner, every hidden door, every secret room.
may you know it all as your own. as yours.
may kindness dwell in your mouth.
may you know how to say your own name with love.
if you ever want to give up, may a blackbird find you.
may she settle in your hair, build a nest called, *grace.*
—a home within your failure.
a cocoon called, *accepted.*

there, i hope she sings behind your eyes.
i hope in time, that you will believe each note of her song.

i bless you with this.

the thing you do not want to let go of

open your hands. give your eyes to it.

let it catch its breath. let it breathe deeply.
and you—breathe. breathe. breathe.

show it your life. say: *i can do this.*
allow it to stretch its wings. say: *thank you.*

send it off with a soft, linen pouch, to which you must add
kindness, and a blessing for a wanderer.

now, allow it to leave if it wants to.
now, leave the light on and a small window open.

this is how you will know

when i enter your walls i will walk on bare feet.
i will listen for God when i go from room to room.
each word i give you, will be weighed twice.
once for me, and once for you.
your joy will be my joy.
in your grief, i will be with you.
i will not leave until you tell me to.
your name will be safe inside my mouth.
your scars will be my map.
i will not use them as a weapon.
i will make a life out of knowing each waypoint
that marks your landscape.
i will know each cave, each crag, each fell.
i will not be afraid to walk there.
where there are thorns, i will go gently.
they are not mine to remove.
i will know where the water flows
and where the earth is bone dry.
from the green of the loch i will carry water for you
in my cupped hands.
i will not stop until the moss greens itself
in all your wild places.
i will choose you in dark and i will choose you in light.
i will be a fire at which to warm yourself and a shelter
from things that travel on storm clouds—things
that hold lightning in their hands.
i will learn the language in which you were taught love.
i will teach you the ways in which i was not given love.
i want to learn *you*—every day choose to find one more

thing that belongs to your life.
when i tell your story, it will be wildflowers in my mouth.
i will not leave you hungry.
i will not feed you crumbs
and call it a feast.
you will be my home and i will choose it so.
i will choose you, and choose you, and choose you
so that others will know.
i will wake each morning to claim the map of your face
with my grateful mouth.

all the ways in which we stitch love together

i want to walk with you until we grow tired.
until we grow old. until our velveting bones remember
how to forget all the old ways
in which we taught ourselves how to speak love.
how we fed each other crumbs from the edge of the plate.
how we lived inside hungry bodies.
how we called ourselves, *famine*—our pockets stuffed
with whatever we could get, whatever we could make
out of nothing.
still, we called it, *enough.*
at the edge of the world, we called it, *love.*

behind my words

i don't know when i learnt how to do this
this soft-subtle warfare that falls from my tongue
how i send words out of my mouth
after letting each one climb rough-shod up the rose-dotted
trellis of my throat, without allowing them to gather
a single bloom first—only thorns
in my defence, sometimes i still speak
with my child-mouth—watch you with the softness
of my child-eyes
she thinks she knows what to expect, she remembers
the things she learnt—how to sniff the breeze
for what she will not receive, and how to choose
a new name for disappointment
i send them forth, my words, covered in armour and sharp
to the touch, they fall, already cutting, already drawing
first blood, already i am winning
i want you to see the *shout* in me, the noise
i want you to know the tough capsule of my heart, that i
will not roll over and play dead, that i draw weapons
with my words
i am not what i want to be, and i am what i am not
and shallow inside the hot sheathing lies the naked skin of
everything that i am too afraid to say. the soft belly of the
things that i want to show you, want to give you

hiding.

when i forgot to eat grace

when the water starts pouring through the ceiling
and down the bathroom walls, before i have even had
my first cup of tea, i forget
to put a strong thing in front of my mouth
          a lock—to hold it all in
all the small things that ate at me last week, and ten
months ago, and when i was six
they all climb up my throat at the same time, jostling
to get there first
          callous and ready to do dirty work
waiting for a moment just like this, i set them free
to run amok
and i, teller of holy stories, climb out of the boat
and sink, like a rock.

how to kill shame

i have seen a woman unlive her life
in short, hidden breaths
the weight of things that had to be hidden
a second mouth on her face

with my life i want to show her:

not everything that is given, that is forced into your hands
is yours to keep alive

they don't tell you that. they don't tell you
that shame stops breathing, will die a thousand deaths
when you start eating that soft word:

no.

folding grace for the things that do not pass

there are always things that cannot be undone, cannot be made what they were before, cannot be made new, cannot be shaped into the thing that you once thought was yours.

even though you named it: *this-is-mine.*
even though you said: *for-what-i-am-about-to-receive-thank-you.*

even then, it might not have heard you.
even then, it might have walked right past you.
even then, it might have gone to live in someone else's mouth.

even though you live on your knees, even then
a prayer might fail at what you want it to do.

no matter how many times you throw it into the darkness
—call it, faith.

i have seen the lack of oxygen at birth, the freefall
down the sharp edge of the earth, the breath
that goes away.

the *no,* which should have been a *yes.*
the *yes,* which should have been a *no.*

there are always things that cannot be undone.
when they find you, you must name them: *loss* and *grief.*
there, the *friends-of-Job* will sniff you out with their sharp noses. they will sense your grief on the wind.

do not give them your ears and do not give them your heart.

if they use God's name to wrap you in guilt do not listen to them.

they might not know the taste of salt.
they might not know the shape of grief.
they might not know the shape of grace.

at least, not yet.

in time, it will find them.

for forty days and forty nights you must grieve.
fill the soil of your bones with water.
flood the earth.

it has been done before.
on earth as it is in heaven. you can do it again.

this is how you start, how you find your way
through the glass, to the place you didn't know existed.

there are things that grow there
and a river called, *redemption.*

and all your life that wasn't what you wanted it to be?
call it this: *it is over. it will never be.*

if they do not know the taste of salt, do not listen to them.
they will stuff your ears and your wounds with hollow words.

they will call it things like:

at least, and *this should be enough for you.*

it will get better, and *this too shall pass.*

it might.
it might not.
this is only the truth.

still, you might call it: *this is what i have right now.*

after the grieving, and long after the cut, a day will arrive on silent cat-feet and it will bring a thin breeze, and it will open a little above your head.

stay there. the light will find you.

you might call it: *it is what it is.*
you might say: *for-what-i-have-been-given-thank-you.*

here, you will learn how to dwell on the edge.
fierce, you will be a wild animal curled up around itself.
holding softness in your belly, you will be all the things that were taken from you.
you will be loss, but you will be strong.

you will call yourself, *peace,* and it will be enough.
it will satisfy.

you will teach yourself how to hold grace in your hands.
first, how to receive it, and then how to fold it.
how to make it fit. and how to give it away.

this is what salt will do to a life and we are called to be salt.

there are things that cannot be undone, but there is love.
there is light. stay there. let it find you.

the folding, and the folding, and the *unfolding.*

and all the portions of grace.

there are thin places everywhere

my neighbour sings a morning song to his grandson.
a small body's laughter finds me through the thinly papered walls.

the mouth of my right ear rests
famished
against the flimsy barricade—the patterned hindrance.

the shape of the soft offering placed in my hands, at once familiar.

the lilt of the tender summons, water in my hands.

it lingers.

how a thin place, *a lack*, is a gift sometimes.

the sacred in the mundane

i find the feather on the bathroom floor

behind a closed door, it lies bone-white
and still

there are things that happen when i close my eyes
there are things that breathe, that want my attention
want me to notice, anything other
than the sharp lines that i keep drawing
around my longing life
—shushing the yearning, hushing the soft lament

for days i think of this, the wing, the warm breast
pulsing somewhere away from me
away from my sure sense, my mouthfuls of sharp reason

the wonder of it

the persistent message, tugging at my sleeve.

praying with my mouth wide open

i wouldn't want to tell you about God
if you asked me what i believe when you are not looking.
i would rather tell you that early this morning
pieces of the world were still sleeping peacefully.
their sighs mossing velvety, and held in that faraway place
we are only allowed to enter
when we put our lives down for a small, holy minute.
when we stop looking at each other. when instead
we slip away inside ourselves.
hidden.
where stretched out
along our own tender fault lines
we are held. taught grace
in a place where we can't fight it.
where we can't keep it from others.
i should have been there myself, but i was being called.
my name
kept falling from someone's tongue. i don't know who.
but i have been listening for it my whole life.
for the sound that it makes behind my eyes
when it lands like a small, white feather.
when nobody is looking.
i opened my curtains to the dark sky
pinking her edges, already peaching herself.
the tender unlived day breaking wide open.
an offering.
how i heard the robin first, and then
the blackbird.

his yellow beak tilted towards heaven. how nobody
has ever taught him this.
he simply arrived, knowing at once which way to look.
knowing how to throw his song into the wide unknown.
how i stood in front of the window
wearing only my skin.
the air cool. and how it was enough.
no layers. no layers. no layers.
for a moment i thought of using words to pray
the old-fashioned way, the way that i was taught
when i was given a God. someone
to bow down to. someone to hide from.
how instead, i closed my eyes, and *uncovered*
i opened my mouth wide. wider than i was ever allowed.
wider than you might let me if i told you about God.
how i stood in front of the window.
how all the hands were open—the welcome
soft and wild.
how i heard the robin first, and then
the blackbird.
how the small, brown wren took over, his voice a bell.
and i, instead of praying, knew exactly what to do.
my mouth tilted, famished, towards heaven
i ate the dawn chorus.

how to wage hope

it has always been this way, you know—people seeing God only in themselves.

there are so many stones about. mountains of pebbles
—dear God, they fit a hand so comfortably.

ripe for the judgement, for the throwing.

instead, we might sit in the company of a tree and listen to a blackbird singing its song—how it wages hope with its short life.

it knows nothing of sharp edges, or bitterness, though they do exist.

we could tell ourselves that this is a gift.

we could tell ourselves that *we* are a gift.

with our soft hearts, we could wage hope
with every moment that is left of our lives.

we might walk past everything that can be picked up
and thrown, choosing instead everything
that can be given with our palms facing upward.

how to leave

when it comes around again, at long last calls your name
you might look up from your plate, the place
where you have waited to be seen, waited for too long
your hunger the size of a wolf moon, and savage
with desperation
you might stay seated, you might
hold out your cupped hands, begging
            for more, for anything, grateful for each morsel
the way that the left has held the soft back of the right
the way that they have tried
to shape the thing that you have been given, into the thing
that you want—fierce in their grip, and failing

at long last, you might push back your chair, you might say:

no—thank you. i have not had enough. i am tired of waiting.

then slip away quietly through the hole in the fence

the fence that you once built with your own hands
to keep the truth out.

a meditation for one who seeks the truth

may all that is hidden reveal itself to me.
if it has sharp edges, let there be softness in the space that follows the truth.
may the fruit above
name the root below
and let me not be distracted
by the colour of the leaf.
and then, when all that was once dressed up
is laid bare before me, let me be kindness
to my own life.
let me carve my name all over my dry bones. in the waiting
let me call myself, *brave.*

you will carve a new thing from old bone

this fear of starting over, not wanting
to hold the word, *finished,* in your hands

you have been given another chance
—a rib bone, still pulsing with life

take it with your greedy hands

plant it in the middle of your new life, water it
say its name until it breathes, until it bears you
an olive branch

a sign

this is how you carve your name
into the bleached flanks of loss

this is how you start over. this is
how it all begins.

Kabul

to sit at my kitchen table
where God eats oatmeal with me every morning
we remark on the way that cinnamon and almonds
make all the difference
and the sweetness of the fat blueberries
that fall into my hands whenever i open the fridge
we talk
as if the skin of the earth isn't on fire
as if there is nothing hunting me
all my choices running free across the floor
white-tailed lambs without names
here, i do not have to hold them up to a man first
they are simply given into my hands, even though
i am made of breasts and a womb

wrapped in a life of providence, i dare not
ask for more.

for the woman i am told is my enemy

i am not at war with you
—though i have been told that i am.
i refuse to be drawn into a battle.
no matter how subtle, no matter how old.
when i am tempted to feel small in the light of your life, or perhaps, your beauty—the way in which you have been shaped, the way in which we are different, i will hold your face tenderly between my hands and see myself reflected in your eyes.
when your failures escape their hiding place, and they will, i shall tuck them in behind my own.
they will be safe with me.
my hands only want to use stones to build cairns
—small altars to holy things.
my mouth is not a home for arrows.
my heart is a fertile place, and yours is a tender one, just like mine.
i will not give my name to anything that will make either of us eat shame.
i will not be given a thousand small wars with someone else's name on them.
if you want to, i will show you all the small fears
that eat at my bones.
afterwards, we will sit by the fire, drink our tea, and knit all the lies that we have been given, into soft blankets
with which to cover our children.

witness

waiting in line to order my tea
my eyes find her hair ahead of me
drawn up silvery into a perfect bun
an exclamation of joy, perched on the back of her head
there are silk-soft tendrils wisping her face, her skin
is a honeyed, velvet map, fine lines leap like shy deer
when she smiles, they shout:

peace lives here!

feeling myself fall in love
i watch her slowly incline her head to the young cashier
her, *thank you,* slips across the counter
like a small gift, rolls like a brass penny
he does not know what to do with it, not yet
in time it will come to find him, still
he lets his eyes be held by someone else's life
and smiling back at her, he reaches into the unknown
and i am called to witness this ordinary kindness
whispering wildly in its outside voice:

look! here is the answer to your prayers today!

at the table she shuffles around to the chair that belongs to
the light, places herself like a holy book
and i have come to sit at her feet
how she holds the cup up to her lips, drinks willingly
and when she spreads the pat of butter onto her toast
i watch it yield to the heat, how she grips the knife

sending it searching into all four corners
i am held close by the tenderness of each silver stroke
the work of it all, how it takes courage to live
and for all the beauty in the world
in this evanescent moment that i have been given, i am
unable—no, *unwilling* to tear my gaze from the frame
of her hands, the shape of flawless survival
each knuckle swollen, fingers refusing to give in
finding their way
how they slowed my life down for a few sacred minutes
this quiet act of worship, a deliberate rebellion
and my eyes ravenous, for the grace of it all.

a lullaby for your own life

perhaps
you might choose
to wrap yourself up in hope
swaddle the small, tender thing
that you have told yourself
will live
you have made a choice to believe that it has life
sing it a lullaby
even if you must make up your own words
give yourself this
even if you were never given what you needed
what you asked for
you are here now
inside your own skin
this is all yours
watch it as it falls asleep inside your bones
then do the same
tomorrow has not breathed yet
and yesterday
no longer breathes
no matter how hard you try to make it
today
it will not be renamed
open your hands
let it go
rest
here, all of you is held.

things to remember in a drought

the rain won't stay away forever, your drought
will break itself into a thousand memories
the wild roses will bloom again in astonishment
at your quiet courage
wrap your name three times around your wrist
lest you forget that you are scarlet silk
your name, a soft thread of hope
even in your hunger
you are an overflowing cup, bare wonder
wrapped in a lucid life, which has always known
what it needs.

what remains of the day is thin and holy

it might be today, or tomorrow, sooner than you think.
the moment will arrive wrapped in a pause.

you might get to say:

i love you.

you might get to say:

goodbye. i am sorry. i wish things had turned out differently.

you might get to press one last, *thank-you-for-loving-me,* into someone's desperate hands.
i was there in the room when a woman gave this to a man.
the memory remains.

but also, you might not.
it's been known to happen.
i have seen it with my own eyes.
the grief for what can never be given again.
the memory remains.

you are a life that is gossamer thin, always seeding itself.
always being touched by something.
a holy osmosis. a sacred transference.

what do you want for what remains of your time?
hitch up your skirt. kick off your shoes.
find the water. the earth. a tree. some moss. pick up a twig.

let the breeze tiptoeing across a body of water, find you.
stay hungry. there is no greater way to say thank you.

somewhere there are wars, but also, the sky is a blanket of Moroccan blue, and you are here to see it.

if that isn't a miracle then i don't know what is, and i have seen a few, thank God. i have walked through the valley and all the way back again with no shoes on my feet.

i know how to make bread from crumbs.
it's easy once you know what *not* to do, what you must leave behind.

you are beautiful just as you are.
you are more than enough. your hair. your clothes.
the lush velvet of your hips.

so much of what we are *told* matters, doesn't.
the things that do, speak quietly. they do not call
from the other side of a screen.
they do not make you wish that you were anything
other than who you are.
still, life leaves a mark, and if you must heal, then heal.
sometimes it hurts. i won't lie about this.
still, you are everything beautiful. believe me.
i have been told by many mouths that i am anything but
beautiful, anything but clever, anything but worthy.
i have made a life out of giving myself new names.

this day, this moment, this tiny bit of *now,* is all that you have. find the hand that means the most to you. hold it.

squeeze in tight next to the bodies of those you love the
most. touch as if you'll never get the chance again.
kiss hands, and mouths, and foreheads, and belly buttons.
hug, and don't let go until they do.

do something with your presence that leaves a soft mark.
a whisper, like salty air on sun-warmed skin.
be the quiet exhale in someone's life.

the place where they can eat *love,* as a square meal.
a heaping plate. no crumbs.

love is not a snack.

and that thing?
you know what it is. i know you do.
even right now as you read my words, it has started moving
on the periphery of your conscience.
listen! it is calling your name.
listen! if it eats your life, it will take your joy as a prisoner.

don't let it. walk away. teach yourself how to close doors.

this is not a dress rehearsal. this is not a practice run.
this is it. your life.

find all the things that breathe. remember your tender life.
stay there in the wildness.
tie a canopy of stars over the ones that you love.
dwell there until you are called.
dwell there in the mystery.
dwell there in the peace that is surely yours.

the root of everything needs love

everything has a root
it doesn't matter who planted it
those days are long gone
it is growing now—here, under your skin
follow it down into your youngest bones, the full length
of them
then sit with it
lift your face, and smell the water
there is rain on the way
are you ready?
what you hear at first, that thing that climbs up your throat
on a trellis of snaking ivy
is not always the leaf attached to the bone
you think that you are speaking with your adult mouth
but a child slides off your tongue
hurting, and spoiling for a fight
follow it down into your dampest memory, the shame of it
then, lie down with it
pull the pale nakedness close to the curve of your hip
it still breathes, still waits for you to say its name
are you listening?
everything turns its face to the sound of something familiar
if you ask it what it wants, it might say, kindness
what it really needs is, love
to be seen for what it is—the beginning
the soft place where it all started, the sharp hook of it all
where your first hunger was planted
the womb of all your fears
everything has a name.

teaching myself how to open a window

it arrived slowly, this word
a small bird in my hand
a struggling sparrow
how long has it taken me
to unfurl my fingers from its soft neck
how long has it taken me
to yield to its insistence
how long has it taken me
to allow my life to be an honest substance
—to hear my mouth, say:

help

to push the four bones of it across the table
towards another body

and not taste failure.

just as you are

that breathless moment
when you see the one that you love
your starving eyes a hundred searching lanterns
your voice a waiting prayer
your life lit from within
the way home
peace

but you

only seeing ways in which you don't deserve to be loved

listen, all the pieces of your name
are already holy in someone's mouth.

quiet rebel

when they told you:

turn back or stay lost!

how you chose instead to eat the sunset.
to drink water straight from the skies.
to feed yourself with the stories of old moss.

and you lived.

a blessing for the words that leave my mouth

may kind things, honest things, soft things
that know how to cut flesh from gristle, truth from lie

find their way past me

as they climb up my throat
on strong, bare feet

brave, may they fly, crawl
—if they must

find the hunger, find the holes, find the place
where everything smells like *giving up,*
there, may they be full.
may they know that, sent out into the world
wearing their dusty sandals, they are enough.

that they are unfettered hope.

something to remind you that you belong

oh, haven't you heard that you must be so careful which words you pick up with your bare hands and whose words you allow to follow you home.
it is especially difficult to make stray words leave once they have rooted themselves into your fertile softness.
here are your peace-lily hands, so unwilling to go to war, so used to pouring water onto each small flame that you are given. all the small fires that are started at your feet.
all the stray words that want to move in, that demand to live behind your eyes, to set down their long taproots inside the wide-open rooms inside your head. wanting to knotweed and snake-ivy and prickly-thorn themselves.
they live only to strangle.
careful! some of them are shaped like the colour pink.
at first, they will taste like late Summer peaches, but once you swallow the first mouthful, they will make you see things differently, and all the little lies and all the stray words will eventually make you feel small and threadbare.
they will ask you for a ticket, for your permission slip to be in the same room as the thing you have always dreamed of.
the thing for which you have worked. the thing that you have kept safe in the warm hollow of your neck.
you are not small. you are not an afterthought. you are not an imposter.
sometimes, feelings don't know how to speak their truth.
what you are, is a beautiful body so big with kindness and so fat with love.
what you are, is an aggregate of miracles.
compassion lives in your mouth, and all your tenderness has

made you tall in the other realms—those deep-water places that can only be found by bending low to the ground, by knowing how much you have failed, by owning how much you have hurt someone, and then, the breathing apology growing in your hands.
there is always grace.
all the ways in which failure is sphagnum moss graciously velveting your bones, always softening the blow of failure for others, because you know what it tastes like.
and you remember what it feels like to be naked and ripped open in front of others, and also within yourself.
and instead of the hardening, the pouring of pretty cups of acid, you chose to let it change you.
how you allowed it to strip your bones bare of anything that might poison.
how you opened the church of your ribs to kindness.
this is a great courage.
you might think that you are not enough for your own life.
you *are.*
everything about you is true and real, and underneath all the second chances, your first name is, *brave.*
your second name is, *i-will-not-give-up.*
kick off your shoes so that the bones of your feet can claim this new place. you are standing on holy ground.
let me give you some new words.
words like, *belong,* and *presence,* and *held,* and *able.*
eat them with your hungry mouth.
eat them until they fill your bones.
until your name tastes beautiful in your own mouth.
until your ears hear nothing but peace
soughing through the trees.

a blessing for a fellow wanderer

may you find love
enough to fill any holes
may you find healing
enough to cover any wounds
may you find hope enough
to keep your dreams alive
may everything that was taken from you
return to you as joy
may all your failures grow into courage
may you find yourself brave enough to keep trying
may you find a soft place to rest
where you can take off everything that is not yours to carry
may your bones carry peace
may your heart be a rich valley
may your name be a home to anyone
who finds themselves lost
may your mouth own all the words that taste like wonder
and no matter who you were, or who you are, or who you
choose to become
may you always be found by the light.

how to dress love up for work

and then the light said to me:

i am still here. please look up.
why have you stopped searching for me? remember the days you ran barefoot through the long grass, through the wet of the land. remember how you used to hold me in your hands. how you used to let me run golden over your warm skin and through your hungry fingers. how you used to lick the fine hairs on your forearms to taste my touch. the tucking of your pink summer dress into your knickers, your legs bald with young hope. the running with arms splayed wide. running for the sheer joy of feeling the wind chasing you.
come back to me my little love.
let's wait out the fears of this day beneath the wide shoulders of the willow tree.
even the birds hide here. even the birds hide sometimes.
everything hides, sometimes.
watch with me as the clouds change shape.
see their slow dance across the breast of ample blue.
how they strip themselves of their fine white clothes, their holy water robes.
even when they weep, when the horizon of their life falls apart, they don't consider themselves broken.
still, they are fracturing as you watch, plummeting towards the firmament, the soil of which they know nothing of.
still, see how they fall. how they let go.
and you with the green of your ancient eyes, how you eat it all up, soak it up into the red sand of your bones.
how you accept the gift.

this is the kindness of acceptance.
it is simply *love*, dressed up to go to work.

a love that says:

here with me, you are safe.
everything about you is safe within my walls.
within these borders you are free.
you do not need a coat.
you do not have to feel your way with gloves on.
you do not need to wear your outside face.
you do not need to speak with your other voice. use the one that you were given when you were still inside your mother's womb—that other country, where all you knew was softness thrumming above your new, unfolding body.
show me everything that is in your hands.
empty your pockets.
breathe at peace.
unlive yourself.
here, you are home.

you have always been loved

love stands at the bottom of the field, waiting
eyes searching the fog of each new day—calls out
to your stumbling feet:

my wandering love! there you are. you have come home!

Thank you for reading my words.

Thank you for allowing me a space
in which to share my stories.

May your days be filled with small prophecies.
May they be rich and full, falling like bells from birds
soothing the dark skies, and may you remember all the
promises that you were beginning to forget.

Made in United States
North Haven, CT
11 November 2022

26545009R00112